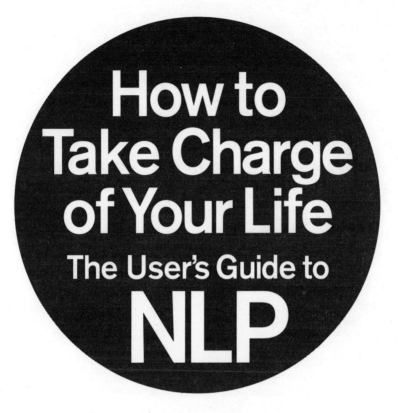

How to Take Charge of Your Life

The User's Guide to

NLP

Co-creator of Neuro-Linguistic Programming
RICHARD BANDLER
Alessio Roberti and Owen Fitzpatrick

HarperCollinsPublishers

HarperCollins*Publishers*
77–85 Fulham Palace Road,
Hammersmith, London W6 8JB

www.harpercollins.co.uk

First published by HarperCollins*Publishers* 2014

10 9 8 7 6 5 4 3 2 1

A catalogue record of this book is
available from the British Library

ISBN 978-0-00-755593-2

Printed and bound in Great Britain by
Clays Ltd, St Ives plc

MIX
Paper from
responsible sources
FSC **FSC C007454**
www.fsc.org

FSC™ is a non-profit international organization established to promote
the responsible management of the world's forests. Products carrying the
FSC label are independently certified to assure customers that they come
from forests that are managed to meet the social, economic and
ecological needs of present and future generations,
and other controlled sources.

Find out more about HarperCollins and the environment at
www.harpercollins.co.uk/green

How to
Take Charge
of Your Life
The User's Guide to
NLP

This book is dedicated to our families and friends for their advice, support, love and encouragement. They make our freedom worth while.

CONTENTS

ACKNOWLEDGEMENTS

This book would have never seen the light of day were it not for the amazing help from the following people. We send out a huge thank you to all of them for their support, suggestions and hard work in making this book possible.

First to our agent, Robert Kirby, for his wonderful support, dedication and belief in this book. Robert is a terrific professional, and his insights, guidance and ideas proved incredibly useful.

Thanks to the wonderful team at HarperCollins, especially Carole Tonkinson and Victoria Eribo, who have been really great in their belief in the book.

Next, we thank John and Kathleen La Valle for their friendship and ongoing assistance and encouragement.

And last but not least, we thank all of our colleagues, the seminar attendees, support staff and Society of NLP trainers all over the world. Without you there would be no life-changing seminars.

From Richard

I would like thank my wife Glenda for her help, her support and her magical smile.

Also my thanks go to forty years of clients who faced the worst and taught me so much.

From Alessio

I would like to thank Cinzia and Damiamo, my world of love.

From Owen

I would like to thank the following:

My parents Marjorie and Brian Fitzpatrick. I would be lost without you both. Thanks so much for everything. You are amazing role models and the reason I am who I am.

My goddaughters Lucy and Aoife, who make me smile continuously.

My cousin Breandan Kearney, a true wordsmith, for his invaluable help with the book. My fantastic friends Brian and Theresa Colbert, Gillian McNamara, Cristina Granizo, Robert and Michelle Orr, Michael Connolly, Paul Kiernan, John and Anna O'Connell, Elena Martelli, Joe Higgins, Lauren Wickel,

ACKNOWLEDGEMENTS

Sandra pou Van Biezen, Lauren Inkster, Olivia Lavelle and Lynda Morrissey for their honest feedback on the book, love and never-ending encouragement.

INTRODUCTION

There are hundreds of books published on NLP but this, and its sequel *The Ultimate Introduction to NLP*, are the only ones that give you the chance to experience what it's like to be a fly on the wall at one of Dr Richard Bandler's seminars. *This book is a workshop between the covers.*

We called this book *The User's Guide to NLP* because through the story you get a really clear understanding of how you can use NLP to take charge of your life.

As the characters apply the skills, so can you. The story is of a man named Joe who wants to break the chains of problems that he has in his life. His story is a story that many of us can relate to. The lessons he learns we can apply ourselves to live the life we desire. These lessons are from a workshop that Joe attends given by a man known around the world as 'The Einstein of the Mind': Dr Richard Bandler.

In the early 1970s Richard Bandler co-created the field of NLP, or Neuro-Linguistic Programming. By studying the most effective therapists at the time, it was possible to identify what made them effective at producing change in other people.

Although traditional psychology has often focused on *why* people have problems, NLP came about by studying *how* people actually change so that they can get the life they want.

This simple distinction has been one of the reasons NLP became a global phenomenon and has been used by millions of people across the globe, including many celebrities, Olympic gold medalists and billionaires.

We have made the story of Joe as representative as possible of the many thousands of participants in courses that Richard and we have taught over the years.

We have learned and applied the insights of Richard Bandler in both the corporate world and the field of psychotherapy, with amazing results.

We've had the privilege to teach NLP to more than 200,000 people so far, from more than forty countries, helping them to improve their lives and businesses.

Our passion, and the purpose of this book, is to share with as many people as possible what we have learned so far: it has transformed our lives, and we want to help others do the same.

Alessio Roberti and Owen Fitzpatrick

How to
Take Charge
of Your Life

Chapter 1

A THREE-DAY COURSE IN PERSONAL FREEDOM

Joe picked up the leaflet from the kitchen table and skimmed it until something caught his attention:

Most people end up having difficulties in their lives and limit how much joy they can have because the very way they think about things and the very beliefs they have prevent them from being able to achieve the best that life has to offer.

He read the sentence again, this time slowly and more carefully. Being able to 'achieve the best that life has to offer' ... Was this not what everyone wanted? He wasn't convinced, however, that the way he 'thought about things' made that much of a difference. Joe knew that his thoughts weren't always entirely positive. At the same time, he didn't believe that the way he thought about things could solve all of his problems. One thing was for sure: any positive change in his life would be very welcome right now. But just how could he make it happen?

Then his eyes fell on another attention-grabber:

Act as if you are the controlling element of your life. When you do, you will be.

While he wondered about the meaning of these words, he left the leaflet on the table and made his way up to bed. He pulled his exhausted body up the staircase and laid his head onto the soft pillow. He had been looking forward to this moment all day. And yet for all the energy that had been sapped from him running around the office and negotiating the ridiculous traffic, for all the weariness that another day had delivered, he was unable to fall asleep. Instead, he stared at the ceiling, his mind consumed with worry. Stress, said his doctor, was the cause of his sleeping difficulties. Joe didn't doubt this. As he lay on his back facing the patchy grey ceiling above his bed, his mind turned to work. He immediately winced at the thought.

Joe was a regional manager of a large firm, and he hated his job. He also disliked his boss, who just that day had dumped a massive pile of work on his desk before running out to play golf. Typical. Joe had also heard rumours about a possible corporate restructuring within the firm. He rolled over onto his side on the bed and closed his eyes.

Then there was the presentation. Joe had been asked to present in front of the Board of Directors in a couple of weeks about the challenges that the company faced. This would have been fine, except that Joe was terrified of public speaking.

Life hadn't always been like this, but happiness seemed so far in the distant past that he found it difficult to remember how it felt. He remembered at some point, a long time ago, being happier, more satisfied with his life and about what he did. Recently he couldn't seem to escape the trappings of work and money. He had given up his gym membership, put on weight and started to smoke again. A few months ago he had tried to begin exercising, but that was a particularly busy time at work with a huge project and he hadn't been getting home from the office until after 9 p.m. He was so fed up at that stage that he had always ordered takeaway pizza and put the TV on.

There was no point in taking care of his body in any case. His girlfriend, Lisa, had left him a month earlier, for who else but a personal trainer – a big burly guy who could lift her in one arm. The anger that he had felt initially was now melting into sadness and confusion. He missed Lisa. His self-esteem was crushed, and he was full of regrets at having spent too much time in the office.

The worst thing of all was that, as Joe curled up into a ball on his bed, part of him felt that this was just the way things were meant to be. He had learned from his father just to accept his life. 'Be realistic, son, and don't take on too much. Failure isn't worth it. Look, there are winners, losers, and the rest of us. You become a loser if you keep trying and failing. You become a success if you're lucky.' But something about his father's philosophy didn't sit well with Joe. There had always been a part of him that believed he could succeed, but life just wasn't turning out the way he wanted it to be.

Why was he so unlucky? Joe asked himself this all the time. His sister, Maria, explained to him that asking why is useless. Instead, she suggested that 'trying hard to discover the reason for a problem is less useful than focusing on the way to solve it. In your life you find what you seek: if you focus on problems, you'll find problems wherever you go; if you look for solutions, you'll find solutions.'

The shrill ring from downstairs jolted Joe out of this introspection. He pulled his head up off the pillow, stumbled off the bed and ran downstairs. He grabbed the phone just in time. He recognized the number. It was Maria.

'Hey, Maria. I was just thinking about you.'

'Joe, my favourite brother, how are you?'

Joe smiled. Maria was the only person in the world who could always make him smile.

'I'm your *only* brother, Maria!' Joe responded.

'I'm just calling to remind you about the course on Friday. Do you still have that leaflet I gave you?'

'I've always thought you were psychic. Now I'm sure of it. I just re-read it half an hour ago.'

'So? What do you think?'

'Think about what?' Joe answered, catching on to where his sister was going.

'Have you registered for it yet, as you promised me?'

'You know that a promise is a promise, especially when I know how long I'd have to listen to you about it if I didn't! Yes, I'll be there. Anyway, I hope you know that I've only registered to make you happy … A course about personal freedom doesn't say much to me.'

'Joe! Trust me, you'll learn a lot of useful stuff. It's about NLP, Neuro-Linguistic Programming. Do you know what that is?'

'I know that you seem to be really excited about it, even if you haven't explained it to me fully yet.' *Luckily*, Joe added under his breath.

'Well, basically, NLP is a system to think and communicate in a more effective way. To me, it's one of the more practical areas of the self-improvement field. Some people call it "the psychology of success".' Maria feigned a dramatic television voice.

'And what can you use it for? Why bother learning it?' Joe continued.

'Well, for example, to help you become free of negative thoughts, feelings and behaviours. It gives you the mental and communication strategies to become happier and more successful.'

'Right. Well, I know you believe it'll help me, but it all seems a little too good to be true, Maria. I mean, surely three days of a course isn't going to fix everything.'

'Of course not, silly. It won't fix everything immediately, but it will really help you get going. Three days are useful to get you thinking about how you usually think, so that you can start taking control over your thoughts and, as a result, over your life.'

'But how is some guy lecturing me about his theories going to help me change?'

'That's the thing, Joe. It's not about theories. The speaker will be teaching you through some of his experiences, and then he will suggest that you try several NLP techniques. You'll realize how it works, and you'll get a lot from it. Trust me, I've attended this course. Now, stop moaning! If you don't go, you won't see.'

'I've just told you I'm going!'

'Well, then let me ask you one final question, Joe. Do you know why some people live happily and others don't?'

'Money? Luck? Good looks?' Joe guessed.

'Nope. It's like Mum always used to say, money isn't the key to being happy, and besides, you make your own luck. As for good looks, it's in our genes, my dear brother. You're related to me, for goodness' sake!'

Joe smiled. Maria had an unfailing ability to cheer him up. He thought back to when their mother had been alive. She had died when he was eighteen. She was such a caring mother, always believing in Joe and insisting that he could do more than his teachers and his father had said he could. When she passed away, he lost that belief in himself. His mother's positivity shone brightly in Maria. Was she the only person left who really believed he could do better?

'Look, Joe, I'm asking you to go along with what you hear for three days and give it a shot. When you do, you'll realize how much you can actually determine what happens. Don't be too surprised if you find yourself enjoying it.'

Joe agreed that he would give it a shot. They said good-night to each other. Moving towards the staircase, Joe knew now that any hope of sleep was faint. He wandered out to the kitchen and opened the window, lighting up a cigarette and blowing smoke out into the cold night air. He looked out of his apartment window and took another drag.

He felt stuck, trapped in the way he was living. He thought about how different his life had turned out from what, as a child, he had hoped it might one day be. He took a final smoke of his cigarette, put it out in the kitchen sink and turned back towards the bedroom, taking the leaflet again from the table.

He looked at it: 'The Secret of Personal Freedom. Three Days with Dr Richard Bandler.' Another line caught his attention.

Our biggest limit is not in what we want and cannot do; it is in what we have never considered that we can do.

Were these words addressed directly to him? With the sentence bouncing around in his mind, he returned to bed. He tossed and turned under the sheets for a few hours. He couldn't help thinking that the course would be a waste of time, and yet another part of him was curious. *Give it a try, Joe.*

Then those dream-like images crept into his head. The images that he'd been seeing for so long now. His mother's face. Her deep blue eyes looking straight into his own. She'd believed in him. Joe always felt that he had disappointed her when he looked back into her face. She would want him to make a go of things. Joe decided that he would give this a chance. For his mother. For Maria. For himself. Could this stuff actually help? It was time to make an effort to change things. The image in his mind of his mother's face changed. Her lips did not move, but Joe thought he could see a smile in her eyes.

He rolled over, and this time he was asleep within minutes.

Chapter 2

DAY ONE: HOW TO CHANGE NEGATIVE THINKING

When Friday came, Joe headed over to where the course was being held and registered with one of the assistants. The man, well dressed, wore a blue badge with the word 'Trainer' written clearly on it. He welcomed Joe with a warm smile. He searched a list for Joe's name, and after recognizing his surname there said, 'Oh, Maria's brother, I presume. Joe, nice to meet you. I'm Alan.'

They shook hands.

'If you need something during the course, I'd be delighted to help you out.'

Alan handed Joe a name tag and a manual, and then Joe walked into the auditorium. There was a stage at the end of the room, and rows of chairs faced the stage. Joe picked a seat halfway up the aisle on the right-hand side. Pop music in the background mixed with the mumbled buzzing of participants' conversations. Joe looked around, confused. The seminar was full – there were about 500 people in the room. The topic of the course seemed to have aroused plenty of interest, though Joe was sceptical. *What am I doing here?* he thought. *This is pointless. A waste of three days.*

He turned and saw the grinning face of a woman who was settling into the seat beside him, then an outstretched hand. 'Hi. My name is Anna. You can call me Ann, if you like.'

Joe braced himself for the social interaction, putting on his best polite act. 'Hi, I'm Joe. Call me Joe,' he said, smiling weakly at his attempt at a joke.

'Nice to meet you, Joe. I'm a psychotherapist. It's my first time here. I can't wait to see Dr Bandler. I've heard he's quite funny and controversial.'

Joe smiled and turned away uncomfortably to face the stage. Anna continued to talk, this time in a German accent. '*Ya, Guten Tag.* I've studied Freudian psychotherapy. My expertise is in psychoanalysis. I find de root cause of people's problems. Don't vorry, though; I von't analyse you.' Anna started laughing at her own attempt at the accent. Her features were sharp and her dark glasses matched her functional grey dress and shiny black hair tied back from her head. Joe smiled politely.

As Anna continued to talk about her job, Joe found himself locking gazes with a woman across the room with long brown hair. Almost as suddenly as they had seen each other, she had turned away.

Joe couldn't look away. He was lost in her. She seemed to have her own distinctive dress style, a summery dress flowing down to her knees. Her air of confidence radiated in every direction around her, smiling beautifully at the two people on either side of her, and in turn drawing smiles from them. *She is way out of my league*, Joe immediately thought. He instinctively pulled his stomach in and sat straight up in his chair. The brown-haired girl sat in the same row as him, about ten seats away. Her skin was pale and white, but her lips were red and her eyes sparkled green like a lighthouse saving a ship in danger. When Joe looked away, Anna was still talking.

The music got louder and a motorcycle roar announced the beginning of the song 'Born to Be Wild.' Everybody's attention was now directed to the stage. The seminar was about to begin. Joe relaxed. *Let's give this a go*. What if his sister was right?

The man from the leaflet walked onstage to loud applause. The first thing Joe noticed about this guy was his calm and his impressive confidence. He was dressed in a strong suit, crisp white shirt and bold tie. After a few seconds the song dissipated into the silence of the auditorium and the man spoke. His voice was deep and warm. *So this is Richard Bandler ...* Joe wondered if he would live up to his reputation.

Understanding personal freedom

Good morning, everybody. I want to start today by talking about personal freedom. This all started about forty years ago because I wanted to help people change. Although I could find lots of textbooks full of explanations of what was wrong with people, I couldn't find, in any of the books, anything you could really do to actually help people change. So that's when I began to search for what I could do to help people become free. That's what my life's work is about: personal freedom.

Joe settled back into his seat. He promised himself that he would give the course his full attention.

Personal freedom is the ability to feel what you want so that the chains of fear, sadness and hate are broken. These chains are made up of negative feelings, limiting beliefs and destructive behaviours.

I began to study one of the most successful therapists around at the time – Virginia Satir. Virginia was skilled at what she did and was absolutely tenacious. She would go after a client's problems and not stop until she helped them change. I spent a lot of time examining how she did what she did, and soon I went around to mental hospitals with her. Because I was with her, people assumed I was a qualified psychotherapist and they let me do what I wanted. You know, in those hospitals you meet some very strange people, and I'm not talking about the patients! I was in a seminar in Seattle, and I asked if someone knew the difference between psychiatrists and schizophrenics. One person shouted out one of my favourite answers to this question. She said, 'Sure! A schizophrenic can get well and go home!'

Joe chuckled to himself. He was pleasantly surprised by this guy's tone. He could sense Anna, sitting beside him, squirming in her seat.

Take psychoanalysis, which is weird enough itself. The idea that your problems stem from the fact that you fancy your mother or father. I mean, please.

Again, Joe tried to suppress a laugh, turning his head towards Anna. Her face was bright red and she fidgeted with her hands.

People always ask me how much resistance I must have gotten from the fields of psychology and psychotherapy, and the truth is, I got very little. Most psychologists and psychotherapists were delighted to learn more useful ideas that could help their clients change. They were good people frustrated with the standard model of psychology at the time. Some of the therapists who had been working that way for years began to change their approach when they found the skills I taught them more useful.

A few years ago they thought that a person's problems always came from their past, but I believe the reason people have problems is simply that they were born, grew up, and learned to think in certain ways.

Many people feel trapped by the past, but they aren't really trapped. They're just practising a habit of feeling bad.

A lot of people have had bad things happen to them, so instead of being glad that it's not happening now they go through it over and over and over in their heads, so that their present is destroyed by their past.

We always have the choice of taking our past and building a better future or taking our past and limiting our future.

That's what my work has always been about: teaching people how to make it so that when they look at their past they learn from it, but they don't suffer because of it.

Joe thought about this statement. He understood what it meant, but how could he make it true for himself?

While I was going around to the hospitals with Virginia, I was asked to work with Charlie. Charlie was a schizophrenic. He believed that the Devil spoke to him. He would tell the psychiatrists and nurses that the Devil visited him and told him bad things about them. His family was distraught at his situation, and they had heard about my different way of working, so they asked if I could help him.

People declared him crazy, but to me he was no more crazy than most of the people I grew up with. People just have different ways of thinking, some of them useful, some of them not so useful. What I'm here to do is to teach you how you can think in a more useful way so you can feel happier and more free.

As Richard Bandler moved about the stage, Joe was completely caught up in his passion for this topic. His hand gestures and tone of voice pulled his listeners closer towards him. He strode around the stage with authority and charm. It was clear to Joe that he knew what he was talking about.

The by-product of this not-useful way of thinking is that it creates great difficulties that manifest themselves in many ways, from schizophrenia to depression to all kinds of ludicrous self-defeating behaviours.

To me, anybody who goes inside themselves and makes their life more miserable than it needs to be is an example of someone who chains themselves to the belief that life is suffering.

They forget that life is not about remembering and reliving unpleasantness from their past but about going forward to look at life as the adventure it can be.

They're supposed to ask themselves more challenging questions, such as: 'How can I enjoy myself? How can I make this easier? How can I make this fun?'

However, today we can go one step further. We have techniques that help make you feel really good for no reason, so that when you actually do have a reason you'll feel even better. This has become the foundation of my work over the past forty years.

Joe started to think about how he had felt in the past and how he felt now.

Personal freedom is also about being able to take the good internal states and the things that you want and being able to manifest them in your life. Freedom enables you to find things like love, success, music and art.

You don't need to have a million dollars to find them.

Some people think that if they have a big car, house or boat, then all of their problems will go away. That's not necessarily true. People should think through what's going to make them happy.

It's about letting go of problems and thinking more about solutions. It's about feeling good most of the time. It's about dealing with the tough times you have and the difficult people you meet with grace and skill. You have more control over your life than you think.

Joe grimaced and thought, *It's a nice idea to think that we have control over our lives, but I'm not convinced. Things can*

happen that are out of our control. But he wanted to hear more.
Richard continued.

How to control your mind

So how do you take more control over your mind? Well, we trap
ourselves by the way we run our brain. As we take information
in from the world through our five senses, we have five internal
ways of representing the information. We make images, talk to
ourselves, and experience feelings and tastes and smells through
which we make sense of the world. It's the way that we represent the world internally that determines how we feel and what
we do. This reflects your automatic, habitual way of thinking.

The way we think and interpret the world affects how we feel
and our mental state at any given moment. To think and act
more effectively and feel more resourceful, we must learn to
alter our natural habitual thought programmes.

Joe was leaning forward on the edge of his seat.

For example, if I were to ask you where your car is parked or
where the train station is, you'd have to go inside your mind
and mentally create or remember a picture of the route to get
to it. If I ask you what you did yesterday, you'd only know
because you'd remember it in the form of a picture. Now, these
pictures or images are unconscious. We all make them, but we
rarely notice that we do. The trick is to become aware of them
first; then we can do something different.

So all of our thoughts are made up of images, sounds and
feelings. Once we become aware of how we formulate our

thoughts we gain the ability to change them. Because our feelings and behaviours are determined largely by how we think, then once we discover how to think differently, we can achieve more effective results.

Think, for example, of someone who annoys you or makes you feel bad. Make an image of them in your mind. Now, notice the qualities of the image. Notice the size, where it's located, whether or not the image is in colour or black and white.

Joe tried to do this. Into his mind popped his boss, sticking his head into Joe's office and demanding that he finish a report by the end of the week because he was going away and Joe was the man for the job. Joe thought of their argument, about the fact that he didn't have the ability to do it and that it was unfair to expect so much of him in such a short time-frame. He thought of how his boss had laughed in his face and how he had told Joe to 'get on with it'.

Now, as you think of this image of someone who annoys you or makes you feel bad, do the following: take the image, and if it's colour, make it black and white. Make it really small. Reduce it in size. Now move it way off in the distance. Notice how you feel.

Richard smirked, as if he already knew the answer. He pointed to a man in the front row.

You, sir. Did you do it? Now, I want you all to really do this exercise. Let me reveal a secret to you.

He whispered to the audience:

If you don't do it, it won't work.

Joe joined everyone else in laughter.

It takes you a few seconds and actually changes how you feel.

Joe focused on what Richard had asked. He took into his mind the image of his laughing boss and first made it black and white. Then, he made it as small as a piece of a puzzle, and finally he moved it as far away as he could. Suddenly he was very surprised to discover that the negative feelings that he had just moments before were not nearly as bad. He now just felt a little annoyed. If someone had told him it would help this much, he wouldn't have believed them. 'That is cool,' he mumbled to himself.

The incredible thing is that the qualities of your mental images can be easily altered, and this will affect how you experience these images. You can also take something that makes you feel good and make it bigger and brighter and bring it closer, and you'll probably feel the feeling more intensely.

Joe decided to try this as well. He thought about a time when he was at an important game played by his favourite football team, and they had won. It was a magical evening. He remembered how good it felt. He remembered the image of how the fans and the stadium looked, and immediately he felt fantastic. He made the image bigger, brighter, more colourful and more vivid. He could feel the elation increasing inside of him. A smile crept across his face.

Whenever you think of something, you make images of it or run movies of it. You can't avoid it. Your brain works that way! So if you remember an experience that you went through, you'll probably imagine a movie of that experience, either looking at yourself in the movie or from your own perspective back then. Those images or movies affect how you feel. That's why people feel good or bad. It often comes down to what kinds of things they're thinking about and what kind of movies they're playing to themselves inside their own heads.

The secret is to take the images in your mind that make you feel bad and make them small and black and white, move them farther away from you and get rid of them, then take the things that make you feel good and make them big, bright and vivid. When you do this you'll be teaching your brain to make good feelings stronger and bad feelings weaker.

Joe was really struck by the logic of this method. This was a huge revelation. He pondered the many implications that this had for his life. Was it possible that this technique could change how he felt about everything?

The answer came from his critical voice, the voice that was often ready to destroy his hopes, the kind of voice that we hear when we think of negative things or we represent pessimistic possibilities. *Don't be stupid. Are you really going to fall for this? It's too easy. Change is very hard.* He shook his head. His critical voice was right. It all seemed too good to be true. What comes next?

Well, it's time to have a break. I want to introduce some of my trainers who will help you during the next few days.

Can I ask all the trainers to stand up and raise their hands, please?

Richard presented each of them briefly. He finally introduced the trainer that Joe had met at the registration table.

This is Alan. He has worked with me for a lot of years. He is one of the best trainers around. Really, he's a Master Trainer. If you have any questions about the exercises, you can ask him. And now, enjoy your coffee!

During the break Joe remained in his chair. He didn't feel like chitchatting and socializing with people. He picked up the brochure that he'd found on his seat and feigned reading it while watching the brown-haired woman out of the corner of his eye. Anna had shot out of her chair the instant the break started. Joe had a feeling that she wasn't sure what to say about what she had just heard. Had Richard's approach challenged her beliefs?

Joe turned around in his chair to see where the woman with the long brown hair was. He eventually spotted her at the back of the room. There were two guys fawning all over her. She seemed not to notice the depth of their interest and was smiling politely as they talked to her enthusiastically. Joe smirked at the spectacle and shook his head. *Losers*, he thought. *Who do they think they are, trying to impress her?* He tried to convince himself that they were being foolish, but if he was honest he would have loved to have the courage to approach her.

'Are you going to talk to her?' A familiar voice came from behind him. Joe turned round … It was the trainer he'd met, Alan. He nodded his head towards the brown-haired woman.

Joe blushed. 'Well, no. Not now.'

'Why not?' Alan inquired. His tone was friendly.

'I will. Later. Maybe. If I feel like it.'

'Are you telling me that you don't feel like it now?' Alan asked with a smirk.

'Yes. No. I mean … no, I *do* feel like it, but I don't. I … well, I'm a bit shy and definitely too nervous. I'll just make a fool of myself.'

'Isn't that what everyone else seems to be doing?' Alan pointed in the woman's direction. As Joe turned back around he saw the guy to her left bouncing around like a gorilla, trying to make her laugh. She was laughing, but more politely than anything else.

'Yeah,' Joe replied. 'But I just wouldn't know what to say. I'm no good with women.'

'Here's a thought. I've met a lot of people who feel bad about themselves, then wonder why nobody enjoys being with them. You have to learn to like yourself before you can get others to like you. Once you do that, the next step is to focus on how you make them feel. Far too often in life, it's easy to fall into the trap of trying to impress other people. Instead of focusing on being impressive, it's more useful to focus on how you feel and how you make others feel. It's important to start with yourself. If you feel good, they'll probably want to be around you more. It's that simple.'

Joe took this on board. He could give this a try the next time he spoke to someone he liked. It seemed so obvious that maybe it could really work.

'What do you think would happen if you approached her?' Alan studied Joe's face for a response.

'Well, I imagine she would just stare at me and wonder what was wrong with me. Then it would be awkward, and she'd make excuses and avoid me for the rest of the course.'

'Wow, that's amazing. You can see into the future *and* read her mind? Quite the skill,' Alan teased, a broad grin spreading across his boyish face.

Joe smiled back. 'Yeah, she would do that if I had nothing to say.'

'When you think about her staring at you and wondering what's wrong with you, how do you do that?' Alan asked.

'I'm not sure what you mean.' Joe furrowed his brow.

'Basically you're making a movie in your mind of what would happen if she rejected you.'

Joe nodded.

'Let me guess. This movie is pretty big and colourful and bright, right?' Alan said.

Again Joe nodded.

'OK, so what would happen if you practised what Richard just taught you and took that movie and made it small and black and white and moved it farther away? Then what would happen if you replaced it with a new movie of you going over there, starting a conversation, getting her laughing and smiling and making her feel good, and made that movie vivid, clear and life-size?'

Joe found the new image in his head, and for a second he felt excited and confident about the possibility of talking to her. As he looked over at the brown-haired woman, he could have sworn that she caught his eye for a few seconds and smiled at him. Then, a reality check. 'It's a nice thought, but reality doesn't work that way,' he said to Alan. His critical voice spoke loudly: *Too good to be true. It can't be that easy.*

Alan stared at him quietly for a second, and then said, 'Maybe reality isn't what you think it is. Maybe whatever you think becomes your reality.' With that, he walked once again to the back of the room as people began taking their seats.

Dr Richard Bandler returned to the stage and continued speaking.

A young woman approached me at a seminar last month. She told me she was on the bus that blew up in London during the infamous July 7 tragedy. That was when explosions rocked London because the underground trains and city buses were targeted.

Although this ugly act of terrorism struck the hearts of all of us who were there, most of all it affected those who were in the midst of the explosions and their loved ones. This young woman stood in front of me, nervously hopping from one foot to the other, wringing her hands, as she told me she had been on the bus that had blown up.

She told me how she had survived but was now plagued by fear. She had not been able to get beyond it. Every person with a backpack, every package, every purse was a bomb. And, of course, sights like those only brought back the nightmare.

She was sure she would die soon. She said she could make no real plans. Her sense of continuity had been stolen. She, like most victims who can't get beyond an event, was trapped in that event, so she needed, then more than ever, a lesson in freedom.

There was a line of other people behind this woman waiting to ask questions. I had 400 other people doing exercises, as this was in the middle of a seminar, so I had little time. I wanted to give her something that would help her feel even a little better about her experience.

I asked her a question that I already knew the answer to, and I gave her instructions that might sound silly on the surface, yet they're powerful enough to break the chains that tie us to overwhelming past events.

I asked her if, when she thought about the event, it was life-size – were the images she remembered as big as real life? She said they were. In fact, she replied, 'They're bigger than real life.'

All at once she began to tear up and shake. All too often, someone like her is told that we must relive our nightmares to get over them. She was a perfect example of how untrue this is. She had been reliving and reliving this for some years, and it had only gotten worse. I knew it was time for some humour.

I asked, 'Are you afraid of trains, buses or planes?'

She nodded, still trembling. I told her that the chance of being struck by terrorism is low itself, but the chance of being stuck twice is ridiculously low. I then told her that I'd like to hire her to fly in the seat next to me, ride in my cabs and be my bodyguard in all my travels, just so I could be safe.

She laughed. I needed to get her laughing so that she could focus on what I wanted her to do rather than being obsessed with the fear she was feeling. People are often afraid of making jokes with someone who has been through a trauma, but getting someone to laugh at their problem is exactly what they need, to start seeing things from a different perspective.

We were ready to begin.

There were two main problems that she had: the fact that she continuously imagined the event happening over and over again and also that she imagined it occurring as a bigger-than-life movie that was happening to her in the present. I needed to get her to change these two things.

I asked her to do something a little different than what she had been doing.

'I know that this terrible memory has been terrifying you, but I want to help you begin to put it where it belongs, in the past. To do that, can you think of the memory you have of where you were after the bomb exploded? Maybe a couple of hours afterwards, when you realized you had survived and that you were alive and OK?'

She closed her eyes and started to recall the time after the event and nodded.

I continued, 'Now, here's what I want you to do. I want you to imagine floating inside that "you" in this memory, and as you do I'm going to ask you to imagine the whole experience happening in reverse.

'I want you to run it backwards so that you see people walking backwards, suck the bus back together so that you see it reassembling and riding backwards, the whole movie of everything that happened moving backwards so that you're watching it in reverse. Run the movie all the way back until before you got on the bus.'

When she got to the start I asked her to stop. I got her to do this a few more times. While she carried out my instructions, I hummed circus music, 'Dunt dunt dulluduh en duhduhdeh.' She giggled. That, as I told you, is a very important thing. I asked, 'Are you done?'

She nodded. I got her to run the movie backwards because she was used to imagining the event happening in the future. I wanted her to begin to put it back in the past. By having her reverse the experience in her mind, it got her brain to think about it in a completely different way.

'Now I want you to shrink the memory of the tragedy to the size it would be if it was a tiny movie,' I said as I held out my hands about three feet in front of her. 'About this big. Look at what happened as if it's in a tiny screen in front of you, and run the movie of that event from beginning to end, but see it small and in the distance.'

She did what I asked of her, with great precision.

'Last, I want you to imagine yourself on a bus, looking at all the other people on the bus with their knapsacks and purses and see them taking pens and books out while they study.'

She imagined this and smiled. That smile meant a lot.

I then asked her to go back to the scary picture. A few minutes had passed, and here I was asking her to do the very thing she's been avoiding and fearing for years.

She just shook her head and said, 'It feels different.' I told her to look at strangers with backpacks, at parcels on the floor of the train. She shook her head again and looked at me, shrugging, and saying, 'It just doesn't bother me the same way.'

Now, it's not that she deleted the event from her mind. It would always be a horrible memory in her past. What I did was get her to stop her past memory from affecting her present. Because I got her to change *how* she represented the memory, she was able to diminish the feelings she had when she imagined it, and it was easier for her to cope. It was something for her to practise, and each time she did so she could cope a bit more. She had learned something that would help her become free from this memory.

Tragedy exists only in the mind as a terrible memory. A memory is just a representation of an experience. When you change the way you represent an experience, you change how you feel about the experience. Now it's time for *you* to get some practice doing something similar.

Joe found it difficult to believe that it was that easy for the woman to overcome the trauma that must have come from such a terrible experience. Richard's idea itself made sense, though. It was true that what had made her feel so horrible was the memory of the awful event. It made perfect sense to Joe that, if you changed the memory, the resulting feeling would be affected as well. But such a dramatic change? And so quickly?

Richard then explained that it was time for the audience to do an exercise. Each person had to find a partner and get each other to think of a negative experience from their past. The exercise involved helping each other watch the experience on a mental TV screen, and then running the imaginary movie of what happened backwards in their mind while humming circus music. Then everyone had to get each other to see themselves in the experience, but with the experience working out in the end differently. Joe wasn't sure if he was going to be able to do this.

He considered wandering out of the seminar room until the exercise was over, but he thought twice about it. He had come this far, so for the first day at least he would do all the exercises. A slightly balding middle-aged man tapped Joe on the shoulder from behind.

'Hey. My name's Ross.' He raised his eyebrows awaiting a response.

'Joe.'

'You got a partner for this exercise, Joe?'

'Now I do.' Joe smiled. 'I'm not sure what we're supposed to do, though.'

'It's cool. I'm a licensed Practitioner of NLP, so I'll help you through it. I've seen Richard before.'

Joe had been hearing the term *practitioner* recently. Maria had talked about Practitioners and Master Practitioners and Trainers and Master Trainers. Joe had felt as if he were in a scene from *Return of the Jedi*. Would one of the exercises involve learning how to use a light-sabre?

'Do you buy into that story that Richard was just telling us? I mean, a woman suffering from trauma? Surely that would have taken a long time to get over. Ten minutes is too quick.'

'Well, I know it might seem hard to believe. I've had lots of doubts too, but I've seen Richard, and Alan for that matter, do amazing things with people. At seminars, Richard taught us to help people overcome their phobias using the same process he used with that woman. It really works. I've met many psycho-therapists and psychiatrists who work successfully with phobias using this technique.'

Reluctantly, Joe was soon guided through thinking about an experience from his past that he wanted to feel better about. Joe immediately thought about Lisa, about their break-up, about the guy with the six-pack. It still felt raw in his stomach.

'OK, I want you to think about the experience that makes you feel bad, and I want you to run the movie backwards. See the sights backwards, hear the sounds backwards and feel the feelings backwards. Go all the way back to before the situation occurred.'

Joe imagined the break-up with Lisa and ran it backwards in his mind. At first he saw the pictures of her with the other guy she left him for. As he ran the movie backward, everything went back like pressing rewind on a DVD player. It went from the constant fights toward the end of his relationship with her all the way back to the beginning of their relationship to even further back, just before they met. It was funny to imagine the break-up happening in reverse. After doing this a couple of times he was surprised to find himself feeling different about it.

Of course, nothing had changed: Lisa had left him. But the pain in his stomach seemed less sharp. He practised the same exercise on Ross, and Ross reported a similar result.

Ross began to explain the details of the technique they were practising and how it works. Joe listened carefully. 'The way you represent your memories affects how you feel about them. So representing them differently in your mind makes you feel different.'

He seemed to be convinced. 'This stuff really helped me. I'm in corporate sales, and I'm happy to say I was the most successful salesperson in our company for the last financial year. From time to time I have to present one of our products to a large group. Sometimes negative memories of presentations that went badly come to my mind, so when they do I just get hold of the images or movies and make them smaller and run them backwards. It helps. I also find that Brilliance Squared works a miracle and ...'

'Brilliance what?' Joe interrupted.

'I'm sorry. Let me tell you. This is a good one,' Ross beamed, proudly. 'Basically, Brilliance Squared is a simple technique that helps you create any feeling you like and trigger it in your body immediately.'

'Right ...' Joe said, with one eyebrow raised. He looked at Ross sceptically.

'Honestly, it works. You see, the secret is that you imagine yourself in the state of mind that you want to be in. You see yourself standing in an imaginary square in front of you. You give the square a colour. Look, let me show you.'

Ross asked Joe to stand, close his eyes and imagine a coloured square in front of him.

'Imagine that the square is full of the colour you associate with confidence. Now imagine yourself standing in that square as you would be at your most confident, looking strong, feeling sure of yourself, feeling powerful. See how you would look. Notice the expression on your face, your body posture, the way you breathe, the light in your eyes, the grace and ease of all your movements.'

Joe saw the square in front of him. It was red. When he built up this image and saw this square before him, he was immediately aware of how he felt and how he looked. He saw himself tall and strong. He saw himself standing upright, self-assured, positive. He saw his back straighten. He saw his legs appear solid beneath his body. The redness glowed forcefully from the square in front of him.

'OK. As you do this, on the count of three I want you to imagine stepping onto this imaginary square and into this imaginary you … like putting a new suit of clothes on. I want you to step into that confident, powerful you and see through those eyes, hear through the ears and feel the feelings. Ready? One … two … three. Step in, and as you do, notice yourself feeling this feeling and this colour throughout every part of your body. Feel yourself filling up with a strong sense of confidence and strength. That's right.'

Joe stepped in and at that moment felt the square delivering to him a new type of confidence. The energy from the square was spreading powerfully throughout every part of his body.

After a few seconds, Ross continued, 'Now I want you to step out of the square and open your eyes.'

Ross brought him through this process five times in a row. Finally, Joe stepped back out, opened his eyes and returned to an awareness of the room. 'Wow.'

Ross smiled. 'You think *that* was cool? Wait till you try this,' Ross sounded excited. 'OK, now close your eyes, imagine the coloured square and step into it. Notice how you feel then. I'm not going to say another word.'

Joe closed his eyes, imagined the square as vividly as possible, then stepped in. Immediately he felt the feelings of confidence rushing back inside him. He felt himself almost lifting off the ground. Stepping out again, he opened his eyes. 'Wow. That was –'

'Brilliant.' Ross finished his sentence with a laugh. 'Hence the name.'

Joe listened for his critical voice but could not hear it. It was as if he was starting to experience things that the negative voice couldn't explain. Joe thanked Ross, and they went back to their chairs.

Lunchtime came, and Joe was invited to go to lunch by Anna. He thought of declining, but he was slightly curious as to how she was going to respond to Richard's critical appraisal of psychoanalysis. He looked around for the brown-haired woman, and saw that she was being whisked away by the Gorilla and his friend. To lighten the full impact of Anna's analysis, Joe managed to rope Ross into coming along with them for lunch.

As they walked down the street, Anna's reaction did not seem as defensive as Joe thought it might be. 'Well, that wasn't exactly what I was expecting this morning,' she declared.

'I'm sure he was just joking around,' Joe said, vicariously offering her an olive branch. 'I mean, he probably says some things only to shock people. He probably doesn't really believe them.'

Anna nodded. 'I know what he's saying, and I know that he's just trying to get people to see that reliving bad experiences isn't always a good idea. I've always believed that if you find out the cause, then you can stop the effect.'

Ross seemed agitated by her comments and jumped in. 'I've heard Alan suggest that the cause isn't the event that happens, but how we represent it. If you change what you're doing in your head, it changes the feeling. Thinking about bad memories doesn't make you feel better.'

Anna tried to argue back. 'But if you suppress the symptom, then it comes out somewhere else.'

Ross shot back, 'Yes, but who says it has to come out somewhere bad?'

Joe lost interest and turned his thoughts to Richard's comments that morning. At that point Joe just wanted to be left alone to think about what he had learned and how it could affect his life. All three eventually settled for lunch and, shovelling his sandwich into his mouth, Joe made some excuses and went for a walk alone.

On an alternative route back to the seminar hall, Joe stopped at a corner shop and bought a packet of cigarettes. The nerves he felt around the brown-haired woman needed to be calmed. He had taken in so much information this morning and his mind was beginning to spin. He lit up and inhaled deeply, regretting immediately his reliance on tobacco and what it had done to his fitness and his body. Now he was a fatty who stank of smoke. His critical voice dominated proceedings in his head.

When he arrived back at the room he noticed that some people were sitting in different seats than before. He moved a few seats closer to where the brown-haired woman had been sitting. If anything there would be distance between himself and Ross or Anna. Unfortunately for Joe, when they returned from lunch they sat on either side of him, blocking his exit on both flanks. He sighed. It was going to be a long afternoon.

Changing your self-talk

Richard spoke assuredly once more to begin the afternoon session. Joe felt more and more relaxed as the resonant tones of the speaker's voice travelled through the room.

Welcome back! Now, a lot of people learn from me how to communicate with others better. What's even more important than that is learning to communicate better with yourself. We all talk to ourselves every day. Forty years ago you could be called insane for admitting to talking to yourself. Back then, if you told a psychiatrist that you talked to yourself he would say to himself, 'Mmm, this person is engaging in self-talk. He must be crazy!'

Richard's movements were measured and graceful. His tone was strong yet genuine.

The way we feel is influenced not only by the images or movies we make but also by the way we talk to ourselves.

Now, most people are aware that if you say bad things to yourself, you're more likely to feel bad. What they don't know, however, is that it's not just *what* you say to yourself but also *how* you say it. For example, when you're chastising yourself, it's likely that you use a different tone of voice than when you're congratulating yourself. It's often your tone of voice when you're speaking to yourself that affects your mood.

Some people speak to themselves in a horrible manner, and yet they wonder why they don't like who they are. You have to learn to change how you speak to yourself.

The critical voice. Joe had tried to silence it, but he never seemed to be able to do this successfully. He had occasionally tried some of the ideas he had heard from TV, books or friends, such as thinking positive thoughts, visualizing beautiful images or saying supportive words. However, his positive voice was almost always drowned out by his negative, critical voice.

Let me explain a little secret that'll help you to do this. Think about something nasty that you regularly say to yourself, something cruel that you use to complain about yourself. Now, notice the tone of voice you use. That's right. Next, I want you to repeat it, but do so in a ridiculous tone of voice.

Imagine the same horrible criticism in a Mickey Mouse tone of voice or a Sylvester the Cat voice. Notice how it feels different. This works because it's the tone of our voice that often carries much of the feeling of the words we use. Lots of people say different things to themselves and wonder why they feel just the same. Remember, it's not what you say as much as *how* you say it.

This struck a nerve with Joe. Was this the reason why he had been unsuccessful in changing this inner voice? Now, as he tried making the negative comments to himself in a Mickey Mouse voice, he began to giggle. He sounded ridiculous, and more importantly, the negative comments themselves sounded ridiculous.

When you use a different tone, it carries a different feeling. Actually, let's do this as an exercise. Get into groups of two. I want you to get your partner to think about a number of situations in his life where he has criticized himself. Once he has identified them, have him repeat the criticisms in a few different ridiculous tones of voice and notice how he feels different. When you do this a few times, the negative voice will start taking on this new attitude, and you will, quite literally, feel different. And the good thing is that the negative voice, after this exercise, will never be the same.

Joe immediately avoided eye contact with Ross and Anna and got up out of his seat. He turned and saw the brown-haired woman sitting only three seats away. He imagined his brilliant square and he stepped into it. Just as he was about to make his approach an older woman who looked like she was in her fifties stepped in front of him.

'Hi. Would you like to do this exercise with me?'

Joe looked over the woman's shoulder and noticed that the brown-haired woman had just been approached by someone else to do the exercise.

'Sure. My name's Joe.' He quickly brought his focus back.

'Teresa. Nice to meet you.' She brushed back her curly hair and flattened the underneath of her long spotty dress as she sat down gracefully beside him.

Joe learned that Teresa was a doctor from Ireland who had trained extensively with Richard. She seemed pretty down to earth and had a warm, motherly quality to the way she talked. Joe also liked her accent, a typical Irish brogue.

'I used to have panic attacks a few years ago,' Teresa explained, 'so I looked for ways to take control over the way I felt. By learning from Dr Bandler I became aware of the fact that when I panicked I made an internal movie of myself not being able to breathe, stuck in the situation, and even dying, and of course that made things worse. Then I learned how to take charge of what happens inside my head. It didn't happen overnight, but bit by bit I started to get the hang of taking control over the images I made inside my head, and I felt better as a result. Anyway, let's try this exercise.'

Joe really wanted to try this one. He desperately wanted to change the tone of his internal voice. Teresa brought him through things first. He did OK at first, but then started struggling with the exercise. The more he struggled, the less focused on changing the critical voice he became, the harder everything was.

'I can't get how this works. I don't know if I've understood the exercise.'

'Can I make a suggestion?' Teresa offered.

'Of course.'

'Use a different tone of voice also when you say to yourself that you don't understand it.'

It seemed simple. Joe applied the silly voices to these statements and found instantaneously that they, in turn, seemed ridiculous. He continued and found himself able to make changes to lots of negative things that he'd been saying to himself. As he practised more and more, the anxiety that he had carried around with him for a long time seemed to become less and less.

Teresa and Joe had a nice chat after the exercise, and Joe made a mental note that he'd like to talk with her more later. She was very friendly and Joe felt that there might be some more to learn from her.

Another break came again in the afternoon. Joe decided against going for a smoke and again stayed in his chair. The ideas made sense to him, that was for sure. But he still felt sceptical that such simple ideas could make such a massive difference. He flicked through the manual in front of him. He had long heard that change rarely lasts and is often slow and painful.

When he looked up from the text he saw, a few chairs away, the brown-haired woman looking across at him. He caught the gaze of her large green eyes and saw her smile straight at him. He held his breath and noticed his heart pounding against the inside of his chest. It felt like his mouth would not work. She continued to smile across at him as she got up out of her chair. He regained control over his facial expressions just long enough to smile back. She began to walk towards him. Before she could get there, however, the Gorilla's friend cut off her journey.

Joe's heart sank. Was this ever going to happen? But there was still hope. That smile meant that she wanted to meet him. It must have. Then, right on cue, the critical voice inside his head started to speak to him: *Come on. Are you kidding?*

Someone as beautiful as that woman being interested in you? Give me a break! Joe's chin dropped to his chest and he slumped into his chair. But then he shook himself and remembered what they had just been doing. He repeated the scolding in a ridiculous voice. It was Mickey Mouse. He chuckled silently to himself. This time he looked over towards the brown-haired woman and beamed a cheeky smile. She noticed and returned the sentiment. Joe then turned back to the manual, a warm buzz in his belly.

As he thumbed through the glossy pages, he thought about the idea of personal freedom. Did he really have the ability to become happier on his own? Could he really have control over his life? Part of him said that he couldn't control what happened to him, but another part said that he could control the way he thought about his experiences and represented them, and that was exactly what Richard had been talking about.

Joe wondered about the extent of control he had over the images and movies he made in his mind and over the way he spoke to himself. If he could just practise that more of the time, then maybe he would find ways to become happier with who he was and with his life.

The skill of being happy

Joe was brought back to the seminar room by the solid tones of the speaker once more. Richard began explaining that feelings and emotions are not things that we *have*; instead, they are things that we *do*.

I often have clients who tell me, 'I have depression,' so I usually go, 'OK, so hand it to me, and I'll have a look at it.' They look at me as if I'm the crazy one. They talk about anxiety as if it goes away and comes back. Anxiety doesn't work like this. We don't *have* depression and anxiety. We create these feelings through what we do inside our head.

Richard paused. Joe digested this information. The audience was deadly silent in anticipation.

If we build cheerful, happy and successful habits, we have happy, successful lives. If we're going to build grumpy, disappointed, depressing habits, we just get good at having bad feelings. Happiness is an activity: it's a skill to master. The more you practise, as with any other skill, whether it's riding a bike or speaking a new language, the better you get. It's the same with when you think about your past. To me, the Dalai Lama summed it up quite well by saying that sometimes bad things happen. The key is that you just don't dwell on them. If you throw a pebble into a pond it makes ripples for a while, but eventually it smoothes out. When people dwell on things too much they blow them out of proportion.

Joe thought about his father, about Lisa, about his boss, about how he had been forced into presenting before the Board of Directors at work next month. He thought about how out of shape he was and how he longed to be free from cigarettes and fit again. He remembered all the tough times he had experienced in the past. But now, as he started to make the images of everything that had gone wrong, he found himself almost instinctively manipulating them, pushing them away, making them smaller and sending them far away, even before they could produce bad feelings.

For instance, being betrayed and reliving the same stuff over and over doesn't help you. I tried it. I went to a therapist, and he told me to think of someone who treated me badly and imagine them in the chair. Then he told me to beat up the chair. He called this Gestalt therapy! He figured that if you take out your anger on the chair, it will help you.

I don't agree, although I must say I do have a black belt in Gestalt therapy. I fear no furniture.

Now, this therapist told me to imagine someone who hurt me in the chair, then asked did I feel angry. He told me to imagine someone else I hated in the chair and asked if I felt angry, and I told him I felt really angry. He told me to hit him and I would feel better, so I jumped up and hit the therapist, and I must admit … I did feel better.

The crowd simmered with laughter. Joe grinned from ear to ear.

You have to learn from your past and move forward, because we always have a choice, taking our past and living a better future or taking our past and limiting our future.

Once you know that, you can get into a habit of learning the lessons from your past instead of dwelling on it. That will allow you to become a wiser person and will help you create a better future for yourself and make better decisions.

For the first time, Joe considered that it was possible that he was actually free of his mistakes of the past and was free to live a different future if he decided to. For a split second his critical voice attempted to stop him and make him doubt himself, but he simply made the voice sound ridiculous. He wasn't going to listen to Mickey Mouse.

It got a little easier each time he tried it. Richard continued to talk about how we all have the ability to look forward into the future or look into the past. He explained that just as trying to drive by always looking into a rear-view mirror would cause you to crash, the same is true of focusing on bad memories.

Richard soon began wrapping up for the day:

The best thing about the past is that it's over. The best thing about the present is that it's a gift, and the best thing about the future is that it's full of wonderful opportunities to feel good. Now, tonight while you sleep and dream, I want you to let all the learning and understanding of today seep inside your mind so that you find yourself operating your brain in a more effective way.

He left the stage to a huge round of applause. Joe sat there transfixed. It had been a fascinating day.

He shook himself out of this trance and remembered the brown-haired woman. He turned around in his seat, hoping to see where she was, but she was already moving and on her way out the door. He frowned. *Probably off to meet her boyfriend*, he said to himself. But Joe remembered Mickey Mouse. He changed the voice as he'd done before, and again it worked.

Anna began talking to him, as he squirmed for an exit. 'What Richard was talking about – that's kind of what we do. We help people feel better about the past.'

Ross piped up from Joe's other side. 'No, it's different. *You* get people to relive the past bad memories over and over. *We* get people to change how they think about the memories so that they don't have to relive them ever again.'

'Well, sometimes we get them to think differently and get closure with the bad memories, just like Richard. We do it through the acceptance of the trauma that has been analysed and understood.'

And they started arguing. Joe rolled his eyes to heaven jokingly. He was starting to enjoy their verbal jostling and becoming interested in their different points of view.

On their way out of the building, Joe went up to Alan to thank him for his advice earlier. 'Thanks for everything today, Alan.'

'You're welcome, Joe. Some pretty cool stuff, huh?' Alan replied enthusiastically.

'Yes, very interesting indeed. I suppose it's really about the idea that we can change our feelings.'

'Of course. The one thing in life that you can control is the inside of your head. If someone went into your house and painted horrible picture on your walls, you wouldn't leave them there, would you? No, of course not. You'd paint over them. Then why leave bad ideas inside your head? Unwanted negative images or horrible voices … there's no point. You have to take control and start playing with it immediately. So what most people do is spend most of their time practising feeling bad. The secret is to realize that you are, as Richard explains it, the driver of your own bus.'

Joe nodded.

'One more thing, Joe. I noticed that you haven't been taking any notes at the breaks. I highly recommend that you get yourself a personal journal. Record everything you've been learning, all of these ideas. Become a student of your life, and you'll learn to improve your world. When you go home tonight, review the ideas that you learned about here. Record them, and you'll be able to use them the rest of your life.'

Joe said good-bye to Alan and decided to pick up a journal on his way home. The cover was brown leather and the pages were thick and smooth. He had learned some fascinating techniques to change how he thought and felt. He wanted to write down the things he had learned about the control he could have over the way he experienced the world. He had gone through life hoping for the best, but now he had the tools for reaching for the best.

His thoughts moved back to the brown-haired woman. He wanted to talk with her. She seemed lovely. But he knew nothing about her. Maybe she was already involved romantically. Maybe she wasn't. Maybe she'd be interested in him. Maybe she wouldn't be. His critical internal voice fought to drown out his hopeful internal voice, but this time Joe and Mickey Mouse had control.

When he arrived home he picked up the leaflet that had convinced him to attend the course. He studied it carefully. *Is this the real deal?* he wondered. Sure, the techniques worked, but could they last? A leopard can't change its spots. Then he remembered what Alan had said: 'Maybe reality isn't what you think it is. Maybe whatever you think becomes your reality.'

That night Joe fell into an easy sleep again. Just before dozing off, he decided that he wasn't a leopard, and his thoughts and feelings weren't spots. Tomorrow, he thought, would be another interesting day.

Chapter 3

DAY TWO: HOW TO CHANGE LIMITING BELIEFS

The power of a belief

Joe picked up his manual and left for the workshop. He arrived a few minutes early. He introduced himself to the two guys sitting beside him. To his right was a lawyer named Mark, and to his left a student and sportsperson named Peter. Peter was a top amateur hundred-metre sprinter and looked every inch the athlete. Mark was in his forties and wore a golf shirt and khakis. He explained that he was interested in communicating more effectively.

'I work in a New York-based law firm. So I get to speak in public quite a lot. Obviously, good communication skills are important, especially in what I do. One of the guys I worked with on a case last year was amazing. He was so confident in front of the jury, and listening to him I figured that that was a skill worth mastering. I asked the guy what he did to become so good. He just said to me, "Richard Bandler." So here I am.'

Peter had come all the way from Munich for the course. He wore a T-shirt, tracksuit bottoms and trainers. His aim was to access and maintain a peak state when he was competing, and especially to keep performance anxiety at bay.

'Most of the top sports guys in the world have their own personal coach working with them and are using this kind of stuff. I thought, why not go out and learn it myself? I mean, I've already studied sports psychology. From what I've heard, Richard himself is the man when it comes to stuff like this.'

Peter's broad shoulders and huge chest dwarfed Joe's squat frame. 'I find myself getting anxious, you know? When I'm competing I get nervous. I spent a year in England competing in track and field with the best, and at practice I was all over them. It was in the actual competition when I let myself down sometimes. When I get scared I tighten up. I need to get the edge in competition, because I've got the qualifiers for the European Championships in a couple of months. Besides, even if I do use a personal coach, no harm in having some extra knowledge myself, is there?'

Joe nodded. He remembered the Brilliant Square that he'd stepped into the day before and thought that such a technique might well be useful for Peter. *Maybe I should introduce Peter to Ross*, he mused.

When Richard appeared he looked just as full of life as he had done the day before. He began to speak, and as usual silence fell upon the auditorium.

Think about this: problems don't exist independently of human beings; they don't exist in the universe at large. They exist in our perceptions and understandings. Our belief in things is what makes them real.

What I'm interested in doing today is just looking at beliefs. If you take charge of your beliefs, you take charge of your life.

Joe listened, but he questioned this in his mind. Surely problems were real, whether they were believed in or not?

Part of what we need to do is help people believe in more useful ideas.

For example, I was telling you about Charlie. He was one of those sweet paranoid schizophrenics, the kind you feel sorry for.

He was terrified. I asked him, 'You keep looking out of the window. We're on the third floor. What are you expecting to find?'

And he told me that the Devil talked to him. And when the psychiatrist would come in Charlie would go, 'The Devil told me that you belong to him and you're going to burn in hell.' And the psychiatrist would shake his head and try to help Charlie feel better by giving him more drugs. This was done in the hope that it would 'clear his mind up'.

Now, I grew up in the sixties and I have a bit of experience with that ... and I never found that taking more drugs cleared anybody's mind up ... at least as far as I can remember!

Joe smiled. Richard's humour relaxed him further into the morning session.

Most of the psychiatrists simply didn't know any better. Their hearts were in the right place, but with few exceptions they were expected to treat everyone the same. They wouldn't try anything new. That was where I had the advantage. I figured that if what they were doing wasn't working, then anything I did would have a better shot. The psychiatrists would tell him that he wasn't talking to the Devil, and Charlie would respond, 'He told me you'd say that. He also told me to say that he'll see you soon.'

Well, what I believe is that if a schizophrenic isn't in touch with reality, what we need to do is change reality. In fact, changing reality is a good idea even if you aren't schizophrenic. Often, we think our own way of seeing the world seems like the correct way, until we're proven wrong. Reality isn't as fixed as we might think it is.

For centuries people said the world was flat, and therefore you can't sail around it or you'll fall off, so nobody tried … for a while, but when somebody said, 'Screw it, let's do it,' they found a whole new world. There were continents out there … and they went, 'Wow! Look at all this.'

Yes, Joe thought. There were many things that he had once believed but that he later found out he had got wrong. Joe began to wonder silently.

How many ideas have I believed in that have prevented me from doing better in my life but that might not be true? How many times have I given up on things just because I believed I wasn't good enough to achieve them? How many things have I missed out on because I was convinced that I couldn't have them?

Joe was beginning to see that his beliefs were the real issue.

The reason I've been so successful with clients whom everybody has given up on is primarily because I haven't given up on them. It's not that the first thing I did with them always worked. I was always just determined to help them through their problems. I think that's an essential quality of anyone who wants to change. They have to be determined.

I've looked at their case history as only one thing: a list of things that didn't work. What I'm interested in are things that do work, starting with the right kind of beliefs.

Take placebos. Sometimes people refer to them dismissively, 'Oh, it's just a placebo effect.' Excuse me? *Just* a placebo effect? What we're saying here is that you have the power to produce your own painkillers or your own antidepressants. And we're not talking about Indian gurus; we're not talking about holy men. We're talking about medical research. Statistics prove that your mind can be just as effective as a painkiller. This comes from extensive studies conducted on perfectly normal people. In fact, researchers know now that your brain functions differently after being given a placebo.

My theory is, let's start building our own placebos in the form of beliefs that help us improve our lives. The 'reality' that you build with your mind, thanks to the sheer power of your beliefs, can be as real as any external agent. That's just amazing; that's just how much power you can unleash.

Joe had heard of the idea that we can actually help heal our bodies through our minds, but honestly he had to admit that he had thought that it was rubbish. He had always believed that it was just medicine that healed people. Now he was intrigued by the power of the placebo.

I've seen people doing amazing miracles and being cured accidentally. One of the people I met, his father had a terminal illness and was sent home from the hospital. They didn't tell him why.

When he returned home he started getting up and going into the back yard and gardening, started doing this and that and started going for walks, and the family kept going, 'He's just going to drop.' But they didn't tell him. Six months down the road the family started getting worried. They contacted the doctor and said, 'You said he was going to die, and he's still alive.'

And the doctor went, 'You're kidding. I thought he'd died months ago.'

And they went, 'No, but his flowers are blooming. He's cooking, he's taking over the kitchen, and he's dating.'

And the doctor went, 'You'd better bring him in. I have to examine him.'

So they brought him in, and they tested him, and the illness had disappeared. They called it spontaneous remission. However, the father was upset. He said, 'Excuse me. Why am I being tested? You already cured me.'

And the doctor went, 'What?'

'Well, you sent me home. You wouldn't have sent me home if you hadn't cured me.'

So it was probably his accidental belief that he had got better that resulted in his spontaneous remission.

Now the doctor ... I had to call him, and I said, 'Is this a true story?'

And the doctor said, 'Well, no. Actually what happened was that the test must have been misread. And it must have been a mistake.'

There are lots of examples in which we face some things we can't explain and make excuses for it. This is where we fail to see the obvious. There are thousands and thousands of cases of spontaneous remission every year.

Joe wondered whether the man's disease had been misdiagnosed. Could he really have had a spontaneous remission? He had heard of the concept before. Obviously many people with terminal illnesses will die no matter how much they believe they'll survive, but does believing you can survive give you more of a chance to overcome a serious disease? Even if it was only a slightly larger chance, surely this was groundbreaking?

Your beliefs can either trap you or set you free. Whatever you believe will determine what you decide to do. If you truly want to change, the first step is to believe one hundred percent that you can and that you will.

Coffee break soon came. Joe joined in with Mark and Peter's conversation about the importance of believing in your ability to create the life you want and how it is possible to change others' beliefs.

Joe paid particular attention to what Peter was saying. He seemed quite sceptical. 'Just because you believe in something, that doesn't make it real. I mean, if I believed I could beat the world record, that doesn't mean I would do it.'

Mark disagreed. 'Yes, but what about Roger Bannister? For many years it was widely believed to be impossible for a human to run a mile in under four minutes. But in 1954 Roger Bannister became the first man to do it. What happened then? About two months after Bannister's breakthrough John Landy ran the mile in less than four minutes in Finland. Within three years sixteen other runners also cracked the four-minute mile. The fact that it could be beaten meant that others believed it, so they were able to do it as well.'

Peter acknowledged this argument with a contemplative shake of his head.

Joe wanted to offer something to the discussion. 'Yeah, I agree. It's amazing to think of what Bannister's achievement led to, but I understand where you're coming from, Peter. I mean, take public speaking. Some people are good at it, and some aren't. I'd be a disaster at it – I know that much. We all have our strengths and weaknesses.'

Peter nodded. Mark ran his hand across his chin as if digesting Joe's comment.

Although enjoying the conversation, Joe couldn't help but notice that today Gorilla and his friend weren't hanging off the brown-haired woman. Instead, today she was alone, staring into space with a slightly puzzled expression.

When Richard came back on, he began talking about music and art.

Who here was told when they were younger that they weren't musical?

About a third of the people raised their hands.

Who was told that they weren't artistic?

Another third raised their hands.

Now, my questions are ... *Who says?* and *How do they know?*

I say this because I was told the same thing. When I was in school I was asked to draw a tree, and when I did the teacher came to me and said, 'That picture is horrible. You just aren't artistic.' Now, for the next thirty years I never picked up a paintbrush, because I believed her. Then one day my wife came home with paints and a paintbrush and said, 'Let's paint,' and I found myself saying, 'But I'm not artistic.' She looked at me with one eyebrow raised. There's something about raising an eyebrow at someone. It immediately challenges them.

I went out to Covent Garden in London and found one of these painters who was talented and skilled. I asked him how he was able to paint the pictures. He just explained that he looked at what he was going to draw, and then imagined it on the page. He did this a few times until he could see the figure vividly and clearly on the page. Then he would simply follow the lines he imagined on the page until he could replicate what he saw on the outside. So I began to practise that skill and found myself learning to paint.

We are given so many limitations from others that it's healthy to doubt some of them. Speaking of that, let's talk about the belief that many people have about public speaking. Some people believe that they're not the kind of person who could present confidently in front of an audience. They think that they're just shy.

Joe felt as if Richard was speaking directly to him. The thought of speaking to a big group of people absolutely terrified Joe.

Now, I'm sure there are plenty of you here today who are convinced that there's no way you can change. I want to do a demonstration because I want to show you that change is possible, and not only that but that it can happen in a few minutes. Then you're going to try it, and don't be too surprised at how easy and quick it is to change the way you feel.

Richard asked for a volunteer who was scared of public speaking.

Nobody raised a hand at first. Joe's stomach tightened. He held his breath and looked straight down towards his feet. From the corner of his eye he saw Mark raising his hand. Joe was confused for a second. Wasn't public speaking what Mark did for a living? Joe's heart started to race. He realized that Mark's hand was in the air but was pointing at *him*.

Richard looked down from the stage. 'The guy to your left?' he said to Mark.

Mark nodded cheekily.

Joe cringed and tried to curse Mark under his breath but his throat was as dry as a desert.

'What's your name?' Richard asked Joe.

Joe's heart rate increased rapidly, and he could already feel his face flushing.

'Joe,' he said softly, the word sticking in his throat.

'Excuse me?' Richard asked. Joe repeated his name again after clearing his throat. He was doing his best to get as much volume as he could, but he struggled under the intense gaze of the audience.

'Joe, can you come up here and help me with something for a couple of minutes? I want to help you make a change with this.'

Joe gulped. He couldn't refuse Richard Bandler, as this might lead to further embarrassment. He felt trapped. His knees trembled as he slid out of his chair and started walking towards the stage. Every step to the stage took him closer and closer to what was certain to be the most humiliating experience of his life. Joe could remember the fear he had of speaking in front of even small groups. Now he was faced with the agonizing prospect of trying to speak in front of about 500 people.

As he walked up, his legs were heavy and he could feel everyone's eyes on him. Then he remembered the brown-haired woman would be watching. She would never want to have anything to do with him. He felt that he was about to be humiliated.

When Joe finally made it to the stage, he faced Dr Bandler. He kept focused on him because the thought of what was behind him scared him too much. Up close, Richard had even more presence.

Turning to the audience, Richard continued.

Did you know that a recent survey stated that the average person's greatest fear is having to give a speech in public? Somehow this ranked even higher than death, which was third on the list. So if that's true it means that at a funeral most people would rather be the guy in the coffin than have to stand up and give a eulogy.

Laughter trickled across the auditorium again. Even Joe couldn't suppress a semi-smile. Richard turned back to him again.

'Now, Joe, you've been scared of presenting for a while now. Is that right?'

Joe nodded. He felt his throat constricting further.

'Let me ask you a question, then: Have you ever been wrong about anything?'

Again Joe nodded.

'Well, has it ever occurred to you that maybe you could be wrong about believing you'll always be this way?'

Joe tried to focus on Richard's words. He'd never doubted that public speaking would always terrify him. He assumed that because he hadn't done it before it was just the way things were.

'Now let me ask you something. Once upon a time you couldn't walk. Then you learned to. Once upon a time you couldn't talk. Then you learned to. Do you think it's possible that you could learn to speak in public?'

Joe couldn't argue with the logic. His throat was still dry. He shrugged.

Richard continued: 'Well, you see, I have this belief that you can be confident in front of others. For example, is it just that you're nervous in front of human beings? If you were presenting in front of a group of dogs, would you still be terrified?'

Joe smiled. He managed a verbal response this time. 'No. Dogs would be OK,' he said softly.

'So the problem isn't the number of people who are in front of you. The problem is that they are human beings. They're much scarier than dogs.'

Joe smirked again. He imagined speaking to a bunch of dogs.

'Now, what I'm interested in you doing is realizing that, somewhere along the way, you built a belief in the kind of person that you were. Maybe that's the person that you thought you were, but now if you change that belief you can begin to believe in yourself as the kind of person that you want to be.

'What I want you to do is imagine for a second the person whom you believed yourself to be, someone terrified of speaking in public, and notice where the image is located in the visual space of your mind.'

Joe pointed a little to his left out in front of him, where he visualized the image.

'Now take a deep breath in and out and imagine, for a second, that you are someone who is completely relaxed and confident in front of a group. Notice where that image is located. There will be differences between the two images.'

When Joe looked at the second image he saw it was different. It was located to his right, a bit farther away.

'You have an old image, which is what you believed, and a new image of what you want to believe. The next step is this. I want you to take the old image of you as a bad public speaker and move it way off into the distance, and then take the new image of you being confident and bring it quickly into the position where the old image was.'

In his mind, Joe moved the old negative image away and replaced it with the new positive image. Richard had him do this mental process quickly another five times. Strangely, after doing it again, Joe started thinking about being able to speak well in public, and he could actually imagine doing it. He still felt the nervousness in his body, but there was also an image of his presenting well.

Next, Richard had him focus on the feeling of fear. 'When you first start to feel scared, where does the feeling come from?'

Joe thought for a second and pointed to his stomach.

'Then where is the next place you feel it in your body … and the next?'

Joe imagined the feeling and pointed to his chest and head, then back to his stomach. It was almost as if the feeling moved through his body, then went back to the start again.

'So the feeling starts in your stomach, moves up to your chest, on to your head, then back down into your stomach. Is that right?'

Joe nodded. Where was Richard going with this?

'Here's what I want you to do. I want you to imagine speaking in front of these lovely people, and as you do I want you to notice the feeling moving in this direction. But as you do so I want you to imagine taking the feeling and turning it upside-down, so that it begins moving in the exact opposite direction. I want you to imagine taking the feeling of fear and, instead of it moving up your body in the way you have felt it, imagine it going down your body in the complete reverse. Keep spinning it in this new way as you imagine presenting and notice how you feel.'

Joe imagined speaking in front of the group and could feel himself trembling. He paid attention to the fear that started moving in his body, then started to practise what Richard had asked him to do. He took the feeling of fear and imagined it moving in reverse throughout his body. As he spun this feeling backwards, he saw himself speaking in public and felt relaxed. He opened his eyes and looked at Richard with surprise.

Richard just smiled. 'Pretty cool, huh? Time for the real challenge. Because I want you to make a quick thirty-second presentation to the audience here. Just tell them about yourself. Here's a microphone.'

Richard handed the microphone to Joe, and Joe felt himself freezing.

'Remember, notice what direction the bad feeling is going in and imagine it going in reverse.'

As Joe paid attention to the feeling, he began to run it in the opposite way. Again, he could feel himself calming down. He turned to the audience and kept moving the feeling backwards. 'Hi. I'm Joe, and I'm terrified of speaking in public.' He said this line so loudly that the audience burst into laughter.

This gave Joe a rush of elation. As he continued he felt his confidence growing. When Richard took back the microphone Joe felt as if he could have continued. For years he'd been scared of this, yet everything had changed in a couple of minutes. The audience applauded Joe as he made his way back to his seat. He couldn't explain what had just happened. But he felt different.

Richard asked everyone to do the same exercise. Joe worked with Mark, the lawyer, whom he had decided to forgive.

At the end of the exercise, Mark sought confirmation that Joe would not kill him. 'Hey, no hard feelings about me putting you up there, OK? I thought it would help you, and you did great.'

'No, I do appreciate that now. It was just what I needed, though for a few minutes there I wanted you to die a slow, painful death and end up in that coffin Richard was talking about!'

Mark threw his arm around Joe. 'Yes, and you'd be giving the eulogy.'

They laughed as they both went for lunch.

Believe that change is possible

Joe found himself eating lunch at a table with Mark, Peter and the Gorilla. The Gorilla was an entrepreneur from the UK. He was loud, but, as Joe realized, he was OK.

Peter said how impressed he was with Richard's demonstration involving Joe. 'Man, he blew my mind with that demo with you. What a turnaround! You were shaking like a leaf when you went up there. And then you looked like a pro when you started speaking. You weren't pretending to be scared at first, were you?'

Joe raised his eyebrows. 'Pretending? No, I wasn't. I still can't believe I was able to do that.'

Peter nodded his head, 'Tell me about it. I just finished the exercise, and now I feel like I can start breaking some records.'

Joe was clearly now the object of some attention. A number of different people came up to him while he was having lunch, each full of praise for him. One couple he got chatting with, however, didn't seem to be so impressed. Neither was wearing a name badge, unlike all the other participants, and they didn't bother introducing themselves.

The woman remarked, 'Well done, going onstage and all that. Though, obviously, you didn't really have any fear; otherwise, it wouldn't have been so easy. It's amazing how many people are gullible and would have thought that you did.'

'Well, actually ...' Joe began.

'Certainly!' the man interjected. 'I agree. I mean, Dr Bandler tells interesting stories, but the idea that lifelong fears can be eradicated so quickly – I mean, please.'

The woman chipped in again. They were like a tag team of negativity. 'Yes, my fear is real. After six years of therapy I finally understood the cause. Now I can begin to elaborate on it and work through the trauma that generated it.'

'Did you try the exercise?' Joe asked.

'No. There was no point, was there, Fred?'

'No point at all, Julia,' he replied. 'Pointless. I've done that kind of thing. The whole visualize-that-you're-confident thing. It just doesn't work.'

Fred was so dismissive in his comments that Joe felt slightly irritated. He'd been through the experience. He could understand why they were thinking that way. He knew that it would seem unlikely to anyone who hadn't experienced it that such a terrific change could happen so quickly, but they apparently

hadn't even tried any of the exercises. He was starting to understand why a person's beliefs could determine whether they were
going to be able to change.

Fred and Julia left the table before Joe had an opportunity to
respond. Joe glanced over towards Peter, who just shook his
head.

'They just don't get it, bro. If you don't do it, it won't work,'
he said, winking.

When Joe got back to the auditorium he bumped into Alan.
'Hey, Joe. How's today going for you? Good job onstage. Feel
better about things?'

Joe nodded affirmatively. 'I must admit, I think there's definitely something in this, but I'm struggling with one thing. Is it
really that easy to make such big changes actually last? I mean,
it just seems too easy.'

'I want you to recognize what you just said. The belief that
change can't be easy will get in your way,' Alan explained. 'By
believing that change can't be easy we prevent it from being so.
You have to change this belief.'

Joe pondered this for a moment.

'Consider this: if you can do one thing that you thought was
impossible, then doesn't it cause you to rethink your beliefs
about what is possible and what isn't? If you can speak in front
of 500 people, something that before today you thought was
impossible, what else is possible for you?'

He gave Joe a moment to digest and then continued. 'Everyone
has potential, but let me ask you, when you are at your best,
what are you capable of?'

'Well,' Joe responded, 'almost anything.'

'Exactly,' Alan fired back, with a massive grin. 'Therefore almost anything is possible for you.'

Joe smiled and looked over to where the brown-haired woman had just sat down. Again, she had a distant look in her eyes. He wanted to know more about what was going on in her head. He made up his mind. He would talk to her at the afternoon break – with his new confidence.

After lunch, Richard continued with this story:

For many years, therapists were too busy trying to label their patients, while I always believed that labelling them was one of the worst things you could possibly do. For example, they brought me to a section of the hospital that they called the 'chronic ward'. What a horrible word ... *chronic*. That means that you can never get well. I think that's a terrible thing to do to anyone, to take away their hope.

To me, it's so important that we can believe in our ability to break out of our problems and become free. Everybody told me that you can't help schizophrenics, but that was because all I ever saw them do was give them drugs and tell them that they were delusional. They weren't chronic patients. It was the method that just didn't work.

Just because people haven't found a way doesn't mean there isn't one. If you believe with every part of you that there is a way, then you'll probably find one.

Richard was drilling the point home: *Believe that you can achieve what you want, and you will set yourself free to achieve it.*

Be careful, because your beliefs can influence not only your life but others' lives too.

For example, there was a research study conducted a few years ago by a scientist named Robert Rosenthal. In a school he took a random sample of some students, and he led their new teachers to believe that those students were of above-average intelligence.

At the end of the year, the students whom the teachers expected a lot showed significantly greater gains in intellectual growth.

Maybe, Rosenthal suggested, what happened was that the teachers unconsciously behaved in ways that facilitated and encouraged those students' success. This is known as the Rosenthal effect, and it shows how your beliefs about the world and other people can have powerful effects on how things turn out in life.

Joe took a note of this study in his journal. He noticed out of the corner of his eye that the brown-haired woman was looking at him writing this down. He pretended not to notice and sat up straight, sucking in his stomach and brushing his hair across his head. What had she thought about him speaking in front of the audience earlier?

Self-fulfilling prophecies

Since our birth, we've been given all sorts of negative suggestions. We've been programmed with a lot of negative ideas. 'You aren't smart enough. You aren't good-looking enough. You're too fat, too skinny, too lazy, too hyperactive, too poor.' We're given beliefs from other people, and the problem is that we buy into them. These are the limitations that are imposed on you. They are beliefs that you must get rid of.

The words of Joe's father played through his mind. He remembered his old teacher berating him for applying to business school as he would never make it. He saw his schoolmates tell him not to bother trying out with the school team as he would never make it. There were so many things he'd been told that he'd never be able to do. He was feeling more and more angry. What if those limitations weren't true?

If a person believes that they are successful, it will cause them to act in a successful way, which will make it more likely that they will become successful. It's what we call a self-fulfilling prophecy. To me, that's such an important idea to teach our children and ourselves: learn to believe in yourself, and you will be at your best.

So what I get people to do is to believe that they're someone wonderful, because when you start believing it you'll start acting like it, and you'll start getting wonderful results.

Joe scratched his head. Many of the limitations he imposed on himself came from his past. Now he was hearing that he could change it all.

He was convinced by the credibility of Richard's words that it might actually work. Joe was even convinced that he could change some of his own beliefs. But he'd been programmed for most of his life to believe that he was just average and could never amount to anything great. How could all of that programming be unravelled in a couple of days? Perhaps he could find Alan and speak to him about this.

The power of self-belief

When the break came, Joe approached Alan.

Joe was greeted by a smile. 'Hey, Joe, what can I help you with?'

'Could you tell me more about this self-fulfilling prophecy stuff? It was absorbing stuff in there but I'm not sure how I will be able to combat all the negative suggestions with which I've been programmed since being a child.'

'Sure,' Alan replied. 'You see, Joe, there are different kinds of beliefs we're talking about here.

'First, there are beliefs about what you think is possible and impossible or what is easy or difficult to do.

'Second, there are beliefs about what you think about your-self, for example, who you are and who you're not.

'Self-fulfilling prophecies are connected with each of these types. For example, beliefs about what you can do – if you've been in an accident and you believe you can never walk again, then you aren't even going to look for cures or try to do all the exercises that are there for you to do to get better. The belief that you can be successful is vital for you to be able to do what you need to do in order to achieve your goal. That's what happened to Richard. A few years ago he was told he would never walk again. He refused to believe the doctors and kept looking for ways to get the result. Now he's back walking.

DAY TWO: HOW TO CHANGE LIMITING BELIEFS

'It's similar with beliefs about ourselves – I worked as a consultant in a social research company recently. They had problems because a lot of good workers left the company. They were researchers who had worked successfully for a number of years.

'The company was bought by someone else, and the workers were called into a meeting with the new CEO, who explained to them that from then on they weren't just *researchers* any more. The CEO told them that their new role was also to sell their research to customers, and so from then on they had to consider themselves *salespeople* as well.

'That created a conflict for some of them because they thought about themselves as researchers, *not* as salespeople, and that was why they had applied for a job in the leading company in social research.

'Even if the CEO wanted them to be salespeople, they weren't salespeople. They were researchers. That was their professional identity. The new CEO had violated their beliefs about themselves.'

Joe nodded. 'OK, I think I understand the point. So if I believe I'm a confident person, that will make me behave in a more confident way. But if I believe I'm shy, I'll start to behave in a more timid way. If I go to an interview and believe I deserve the job, then I have a much better chance of getting it.'

'Yes, of course. What you believe determines how you act. How you act determines what results you get, and the results you get determine what your beliefs are. It's a cycle: beliefs, actions, results, beliefs.'

'OK. Thanks, Alan. That makes sense. But how can I possibly change *all* of my limiting beliefs?'

Change your limiting beliefs

'Well, the exercise that Richard led you through, the one where you change the location of the picture, and so on – that's one way. Another way is to ask yourself some questions about the beliefs. For example, give me an example of a limiting belief you have.'

Joe struggled for a second, and then said, 'I suppose, just generally, that I'll never amount to anything.'

'OK, then let me ask you this. How do you know this?'

'Because I was told that, and I haven't amounted to much so far in life.'

'Is it possible that whoever told you that was wrong? Could they have made a mistake?'

'Yeah, of course, but they seem to have been proven correct.'

'And how have you tried to be "something" in the past?'

Joe racked his brains.

Alan looked at him. 'Let me guess. Each time you had the chance to become something you reminded yourself of what you'd been told, so you didn't try or you failed to be at your best.'

Joe couldn't answer. Had he limited himself with voices from the past? Joe felt a shiver go up and down his spine.

'So challenge your beliefs with questions like "How do you know that's true?" and "Who said that? Could they have been wrong?" When you ask questions like this, you'll be challenging the beliefs that are stopping you from being as great as you can be. Remember, your beliefs limit or expand your world.'

'Thanks again, Alan.'

'You're welcome, Joe.' Alan nodded towards the brown-haired woman. 'Now, no time like the present.'

Joe turned and purposefully strode towards her. Along the way his critical voice started to creep in, so he changed its tone and neutralized it. He found himself imagining her rejecting him and him acting stupid, so he made the images small and pushed them away. He noticed the feeling of fear and turned it upside-down, spinning it in the opposite direction. The woman was talking to Anna. This was a perfect opportunity.

'Hey, Anna,' Joe said, 'how are you doing today?' He smiled at them both. The brown-haired woman smiled back. His heart raced.

Anna chirped in response. 'Good. I mean, I don't have to believe absolutely everything Richard says, but there are plenty of useful ideas there. By the way, this is Sarah. Sarah, this is Joe.' Anna then looked at the two of them and somewhat unsubtly excused herself and then went off for some coffee.

Joe thought about how pretty Sarah was now that he was right up beside her. Her skin looked smooth and white. He scrambled in his head for something to say but thankfully her soft voice began the conversation.

'Are you enjoying the course?'

Joe hid the nerves and managed to get some words out. 'Yeah, I must say I've been surprised that a lot of the ideas actually seem to work so well. I was a bit of a sceptic.'

'You didn't seem that way onstage. Well done on getting up there. It would have terrified me.'

Joe was about to correct her and insist that he didn't volunteer but was volunteered by someone else, and that he was terrified, but he realized that this was hardly going to impress her. 'Ah, yeah, well, it was great to get the chance to be worked on.'

'You had the whole crowd in the palm of your hand,' she joked, her whole face lit up.

He blushed. 'I don't know about that, but I definitely did better than I thought I would.' He couldn't think of what to say next, but Richard Bandler interrupted the slightly awkward silence as he returned to the stage.

'Lovely to meet you, Sarah. See you around.'

Sarah smiled back. 'Not if I see you first.'

There was something in the way she joked that filled him with butterflies. Was she flirting with him? Joe just smiled at her again and made his way back to his seat. How was he expected to concentrate on what Richard was saying after that little conversation?

But when Richard began, he resumed the story of Charlie, and Joe was immediately absorbed.

So I was telling you earlier about Charlie. Well, Charlie was one of my favourite cases. Every night, the Devil came to Charlie and talked to him.

I asked him, 'How do you know it's the Devil?' I don't think anybody had ever asked him that. Everybody kept saying it wasn't.

And he said, 'Well, I know it's the Devil because he has horns!'

So I said, 'Well, if I came in tomorrow and I had horns, would I be the Devil?'

And he said, 'No, you're too short.'

And I said, 'I beg your pardon?'

And he said, 'Yeah, the Devil is about sixty feet tall. His face is the same height as the window.'

Joe liked how Richard described the characters when he was conjuring up the scene.

And I said, 'What colour is it?'

And he went, 'Red.'

And I wrote *Red*. Of course the Devil's red!

'He yells at me all the time. He tells me bad things about my childhood and the bad things I did. And he tells me I'm going to burn in a lake of fire for eternity, and he's going to peel my skin off.' And he burst into tears and started to cry.

It was heartbreaking seeing him so upset. The reason I began to try some unconventional methods is because I couldn't bear seeing people in pain like that. Charlie was suffering because he was trapped in his own mind. I felt so sorry for him that I decided to do something and picked up the telephone.

I called the guys at my lab because at the time I had an R&D company, and we were doing all sorts of cool things with holograms, so I had an idea. I called them up and said, 'Break out the truck!'

They asked, 'What do we need?'

And I said, 'Hydraulics. We need a big laser, and we need a smoke machine.'

Then the moment of truth came as the sun went down. One of my guys rolled a wagon into the middle of this field and put the smoke machine on, so that you could see the laser. We had purchased from another company a big hologram of the Devil: a big, nasty-looking red devil, hideous face with big, gleaming teeth and giant, demonic eyes. He was red and, most importantly, he had horns!

Laughs from the audience again. Joe tried to imagine what this devil figure looked like. He was a little shocked that Richard had really done something like that. It struck him that the guy was creative in the ways in which he tried to help his clients.

Charlie was just about to go to sleep. You know, he usually didn't sleep well, for obvious reasons, and he was having trouble falling asleep that night. All of a sudden, a bright light shone through the window, and Charlie sat up.

Now, we were actually right in the next room, watching him on camera, trying not to laugh too hard, because when Charlie sat up he went, 'What the hell?'

The look on his face was absolutely priceless. He looked terrified, and he hit the nurse's button. You know, if you're attacked by demonic forces, the defence you really need is a night nurse!

Joe laughed so hard his eyes were watering.

Man, he hit that button like you wouldn't believe, and he was screaming and screaming. From that position, all of a sudden he lifted his gaze and looked outside, and there it was: the big sixty-foot Devil.

He got off the bed, walked nervously across the room, and looked out of the window.

And then the voice came, two Marshall amps, up in the trees, lots of reverb – you can't do religious or demonic figures without reverb. I began to speak ... because it was me, in case any of you were worrying about that. So I went, 'Chaaarlieee!!!'

And he was shaking like a leaf. He wanted to run, but he was locked in, so he wasn't going anywhere. But as he started to make for the exit, I went, 'Chaaarlieee, you've been talking about me.'

Now, he's schizophrenic, and being schizophrenic doesn't mean you're stupid, OK? So he walks to the window and goes, 'You look different tonight.'

Now, this clears it all up for me, 'cause he's not so crazy that he can't tell the difference between this and what's in his head.

Richard was completely animated now, moving about the stage as he performed the story. His descriptions were vivid and sharp.

So I say, 'That's right. That's because I've come for the last time!'

And worriedly, he went, 'Last time?' because that could have a couple of implications, if you think about it.

And the Devil said, 'Now, you're never going to mention my name. Ever again. For the rest of your life. Or you'll suffer unbelievable pain and torture for all of eternity. Do you understand?'

And he yelped, 'Yessss!'

By the way, when I did this kind of thing, I learned some very important lessons. One was to always make sure you let the staff know what you're doing. Apparently that night there were a lot of people in the hospital chapel praying quite intensely.

Another bout of laughter from the captivated audience.

Charlie had been given up on, but to me the most important thing you can do is find a way out of your problems. No matter how impossible the odds, you can always find a way when you believe that you can do amazing things. I find this a lot with people. There's always a way. And just because you hear a voice, that doesn't mean you have to listen to it. It's about learning to change your focus from the limiting ideas to more resourceful beliefs.

Richard continued to discuss how much one's belief in what's possible is vital for achieving great results. Joe had heard before about people thinking positively, but nothing similar to what he was listening to now. What he was hearing made more sense. When you believe in something, it gives you an incredible strength that can help you achieve more than you can imagine.

At the end of the day, Joe watched Sarah leave the auditorium. He really wanted to talk to her, so he grabbed his things and followed her out.

She noticed him. 'Hey, Joe, what the devil did you think of that?' She smiled.

Joe laughed. 'I thought it was one hell of an afternoon session.'

As they walked out, they passed Alan, who simply gave Joe a knowing nod.

Joe continued. 'Yeah, I'm sure there are people who might challenge his methods but I must say, I think I really get him.'

She smiled again and gently brushed his arm. 'Really? I didn't think you did, Mr "I'm a Terrible Public Speaker",' she teased.

Joe laughed. 'All right, smart-ass. We can't all be perfectly open like you.'

Sarah raised her eyebrows in mock arrogance. 'No, I guess "we" can't!'

They continued chatting as he walked her outside. Unsure of which direction she was heading, he decided to be bold. 'Would you like to get a coffee with me?'

Sarah looked at her watch and shook her head. 'Sorry. Someone's actually picking me up here.' She pointed across to the road. 'Oh, there he is. Rain check, OK?'

Joe's hopes dissolved in a second. 'Yeah, cool.'

'Sorry.' She looked pained. 'I'll see you tomorrow, and we'll sit together then.'

'Not if I see *you* first.' Joe quipped back, doing what he could to hide his disappointment.

Sarah smiled again and skipped over to the kerb where the exceptionally flashy car was waiting. In it sat a well-dressed, athletic and attractive guy in the driver's seat. Sarah jumped in and the car sped off.

Joe stopped at the coffee shop anyway. He ordered a caffè latte and sat down. As he looked out onto the street through the window he saw Alan walking past. He tapped on the window to get his attention.

Alan mouthed *hi* and walked in. 'Hey, Joe. What are you doing? Where's your lady friend?'

'She's gone home with her boyfriend.'

Alan frowned. 'Really? That's not good.'

Joe shrugged.

'Do you mind if I join you?'

'Not at all.' Alan ordered a black coffee and sat beside Joe, facing the window. 'You know, Joe, I've seen a lot of people come to these trainings over the years, and there are certain things I've learned from them. You have people who come to turn their whole lives around and expect that at the end of the three days everything will be different. Then you have people who come to meet other people and hope they'll build better networks or even find friends or a partner out of it. You also have people who come to find some useful tools that'll make their lives better than they are or help other people improve their life.

'Richard always describes what he teaches as an attitude. It's an attitude of the curiosity Richard displays, the determination he demonstrates and the creativity he uses. It's an attitude that says, "Whatever you want to achieve, believe it's possible and it will be easier to achieve it." It's an attitude that explains that we can have freedom over the things that limit us.'

'But how come not everyone gets it?' Joe asked.

'A better and more useful question is how can you make sure that *you* get it? I was once sitting where you've been sitting in the training course, and I had a bunch of problems. I was unsatisfied with where I was in life, and I just seemed to be stuck in a rut.

'A friend suggested I go to an NLP course, so I learned more about the ideas, took some courses, read some books, and, most importantly, I applied it all to my life. Thanks to that, I changed the way I thought and felt about certain things. I worked on some limiting beliefs, and I started to design my future by taking back control over what I wanted. Of course, it wasn't just smooth sailing from then on, but I had practical tools and a different attitude.

'I used to believe I was unattractive and not very bright. Once I changed those beliefs I enjoyed an amazing liberation. I realized that the kind of life to which I had resigned myself wasn't the only option. I could learn to be happy and successful.'

Alan spoke with passion and conviction. Joe listened attentively.

'Researchers say that success is not based on intelligence,' Alan continued. 'There are plenty of people who might be called stupid but are successful, and there are plenty of intelligent people who are not doing very well at all. In fact, there are lots of very intelligent people who work for people who aren't regarded as intelligent.'

Joe thought about this. He could come up with plenty of examples of people he knew who fit into that last category.

'The question we want to ask is, what makes one person happy and successful and another not? Since it doesn't depend on your intelligence, what else could it be?'

'Goal setting?' Joe asked.

'Well, that's one thing, but it's not the only one. Tomorrow you'll be learning about setting goals in the most effective way.

But to me, after years in this field, I believe that the real secret that separates successful people from everyone else is their beliefs.

'You see, when we set out to achieve a goal there are obviously obstacles in our way. The main obstacles we face, however, are those in our own minds. They're the beliefs, as Richard explained today.

'What successful people have is a lot of useful beliefs about themselves, the goals they want to achieve and the resources they have to achieve it. They believe that they *can* have what they want, and they believe that they deserve it. This is what allows them to take massive action, which gets them results.'

Joe put his hands on his chin and sat forward so his elbows were leaning on the table.

'What Richard has been teaching you today is all about how you can take control over your beliefs and start believing in yourself more. Beliefs are extraordinarily powerful. You can choose what you believe. So you have spent the last two days – and you'll spend one more tomorrow – listening to someone I regard as one of the greatest minds of our time. He's not everybody's cup of tea, as he often says himself ... but he exemplifies an attitude that can transform your life if you adopt it. I often see people worshipping Richard, but that's not the point. He doesn't want that. He wants you to get the point, which is to take the attitude and techniques he discovered and use them. Does that make sense?'

Of course it made sense. So much so, in fact, that Joe felt a little scared of the possibilities. 'But what about all the time I wasted before this?'

'There's no such thing as wasted time. There are only the things that happened to bring you to the threshold where you needed to change. Then you made a decision.'

Joe and Alan chatted more, and Joe realized he was more like Alan than he thought. Joe wanted to feel, in his life, Alan's confidence and in particular his happiness in who he was.

'Now, tomorrow you're going to learn more about goals and directions in your life. It's the next step in creating the life you want,' Alan said.

The future was something that Joe had never wanted to think about. But now, considering all the progress he'd made over the last two days, he was becoming more hopeful. He promised himself that he would work hard to get as much as he could from the final day if he was to turn his life around.

When he arrived home later, Joe began to write down some ideas that he'd learned that day. Rain starting to beat hard against the window in his kitchen and he moved across to look out at the city. The night was dark, as it had been a few nights ago before he had begun on the course, but it no longer felt as dismal as it had seemed before. This time he looked higher into the sky above him and he noticed something bright. It was the stars, and they burned powerfully and brightly in his eyes. Was his mother watching him?

Joe caught his reflection in the window. He stared at the figure looking back at him. Alan's voice popped into his head. Joe closed his eyes: *Your beliefs limit or expand your world.*

Chapter 4

DAY THREE: HOW TO CREATE THE LIFE YOU WANT

On the final day of the course Joe woke up in a good mood and with a real sense of hope. There were possibilities out there. But he wondered: *Where should I start?*

When Joe arrived at the auditorium he ran into Teresa. They decided to sit together. Joe put his jacket on the seat at the other side of him in the hope that Sarah would decide to follow through on her suggestion of the evening before.

Teresa explained that she was taking the course because it might help her in dealing with her patients. 'You'd be amazed at how many of my patients have health problems with stress having played a factor. A lot of them feel stressed about the past or worried about the future. That comes down to them either remembering bad experiences from the past over and over again or imagining things going wrong in the future.'

Joe responded, 'Yes, it was fascinating to hear about the placebo effect. Do you agree that beliefs can really be that powerful?'

Teresa nodded. 'Absolutely. The more I've read about and listened to Richard, the more I've started to change things so that now I'm more focused on keeping people healthy instead of just trying to heal them when they get sick. A healthy attitude and healthy behaviours are what most people need.'

Making people feel good

Teresa was interrupted as Richard walked onstage again. Joe looked towards the doors of the auditorium. Still no sign of Sarah yet. Richard looked out at the audience.

What I want to do today is talk more about getting to the kind of things that you want. Once you've learned to take more control over your mind and the way you think and feel, then you're in a position where you can start making real progress. Changing your beliefs will allow you to change your reality and will make a new world possible. Now, the next question is, how do you make this new world a reality?

Richard walked slowly from one side of the stage to the other.

Now, what I'm interested in is not in you setting goals, but in you beginning to set new directions to go in. The difference between the two is simple. Setting a goal is about deciding on something you want to achieve. To truly build a better life, you need to make sure you're making continuous progress. You need to ensure that you're achieving the goals you set, for the person you'll become as a result of achieving them. Certain goals will change you and the kind of person you are. Setting a direction that allows you to successfully achieve many of your goals is important. The most essential thing is that once you've achieved your desired result your journey has to continue. Your direction has to be something that keeps you going towards a better future. What you become is more valuable than what you get.

'I'm talking about making sure you start designing your destiny. To do this, however, you need to think smart, and when you're overwhelmed with bad feelings or emotions, that's not when you're the smartest.

Sometimes, depressed people come to me and tell me that life is awful, that everything is screwed up. One guy I worked with said, 'My girlfriend's left me, my parents hate me, I lost my job. Everything is just terrible; even my dog ran away.' I'm thinking if I was his dog I'd run away too!

Joe chuckled and looked across to Teresa, who was giggling with her hand over her mouth.

Then I go, 'Well, you know, what could you do to make yourself happier?'

And he thinks about it for two seconds and says, 'Nothing!'

And I go, 'Well, think of some time in your past when you felt good.'

He goes, 'I can't. Nothing. Everything is awful; life is terrible.'

And I go, 'You know, well, what would you like to do?'

And he goes, 'Nothing! I don't want to do anything!'

One of my depressed clients said that she lived alone for sixteen years because she couldn't meet anybody. She had no friends, and she told me, 'I'm a loner.'

And I said, 'OK, you're saying that you never meet anybody. You don't talk to anybody at work, and you never just go out and meet people even to say hello?'

She claimed that they wouldn't like her, so there was no point in doing it. I discovered that the decisions she was making were based on thinking that because she felt bad in the past she'd have to feel bad in the future, and that simply isn't true. Her bad feelings caused her to make bad decisions, which caused her more problems.

Sometimes Joe was in a good mood and felt as if he could easily talk to lots of people, but most of the time he felt stuck in a rut. The idea of talking to anyone made him feel anxious.

But anyway, her name was Laura, and I gave Laura a bunch of tasks. I wrote them on a piece of paper. I wanted her to go out and just walk up and look at five people and decide which of the five would be the most fun to be around. Then I wanted her to imagine what she could do to make that person think that she was fun. To her, that seemed impossible. She went, 'I can't even imagine going out and doing that.'

And I said, 'Of course you can't imagine that ... in *this state*.'

Richard seemed to be defining the state a person is in as being how that person feels at a certain moment in time.

So I got her to go into a relaxed state, and when she relaxed I had her go back and remember when she was a child, when she giggled and when she laughed, then I had her spin that feeling inside of her. I had her bring the image closer and intensify the feeling. When she did this she could imagine feeling relaxed and chatting happily to other people.

Joe remembered the day before when he'd been onstage. He recalled how powerfully his feelings changed when he had spun them in the opposite direction. It made sense that they would intensify when you spin them in the right direction.

Here is Laura. She's a professor at a university, and she can't meet anyone? Excuse me! She's in the middle of the Bay Area with nearly 7.4 million people. There are more than 6 billion people on the planet, and she can't meet one? Excuse me; that's hard for me to take seriously. When she goes, 'Well, I just can't meet people,' well, that means I am able to 'not meet people'. It doesn't mean it is impossible. It just means that if you're clever and you shape your stupidity just right, you can avoid hundreds of human beings per day. On a daily basis, you have to structure your life so that you don't talk to anyone. You teach class and don't notice anyone's stare.

Richard was convincing in making the state of loneliness sound like something difficult to achieve. Was he right? To be lonely, you had to do a number of things. Were a lot of Joe's problems caused by what he'd been doing?

She's got money, she lives in a nice house, so she's got a nice place to hide. She goes to restaurants and sits by herself and goes, 'I'm all by myself.' And she looks at other people by themselves and goes, 'Why don't they talk to me?' Think about people who are known as wallflowers. To me, they're just lazy.

People tell me, 'When I sit at dances, nobody asks me to dance.'

I go, 'You're so cruel! You – how can you say that? You know how bad it feels to be on your own, and yet you leave other people with those bad feelings and don't help them. What a selfish person you are.'

And they go, 'Wow, I never thought about it that way.'

Get out there. Be nice to people! The next time you'll hesitate, you'll end up waiting … then hesitating … and then waiting, and then waiting, and then you'll die. Alone! No cats. Cats will run away. And cats pretty much like anyone with a can opener. But not you. You'll hold up a can opener, and the cat will look at you and go, 'It's not worth it.'

More laughter. Joe laughed as well but also found Richard's story was striking a nerve. He became emotional and felt tears welling up in his eyes. Far too often, Joe had found himself too lost in his own thoughts to make contact with other people.

Instead of shaping stupidity, I want you to start to shape your life in a positive direction so that you don't just set goals and achieve them, but you make sure everything that you do makes your whole life better exponentially.

Sarah sat down beside Joe. He did not look at her but quickly wiped his eyes without letting her see. He continued to look up at Richard.

Sarah whispered in his ear, 'Did I miss anything good?'

Joe whispered back, 'He just revealed the most important secret to having eternal happiness and a life full of riches, and he said he isn't going to repeat it.'

Sarah giggled quietly, 'So what is it, then?'

Joe looked around at her and zipped his mouth closed. 'I can't tell you, because he swore me to silence.'

'Come on. Please? I'll be your best friend.'

'Actually, if you are exceptionally nice to me for the rest of the day then maybe I'll fill ya in.'

'What if I ask someone else?' she asked, still laughing.

'Then they'll probably lie to you, as Richard told them to. I'm the only one you can trust.' He winked at her.

Sarah looked at him in mocking suspicion, smiled, and turned back towards Richard.

Making what you want more real

Now, what I want you to do is to start focusing on what you want. Typically there are lots of ways to get what you don't want but only a few ways to get what you do want. For example, I had a client once who told me that he wanted to lose twenty-five pounds. I asked him what he wanted to have, but he kept telling me he wanted to lose twenty-five pounds.

So I left the room for a minute and came back with my chainsaw and told him, 'OK, it'll hurt for only a little while.' I asked him how much he thought his arm weighed. It was only when I turned on the chainsaw, though, that he realized what I was doing. He looked at me as if I was crazy. But all I was doing was giving him an option by which he could lose twenty-five pounds.

Joe grinned at the thought of Richard handling the chainsaw. The message was clear. Losing twenty-five pounds was a poor goal.

Two useful questions to help a person set up an effective goal are: What do you want? And how will you know when you've achieved it? This will help you transform a lousy goal into a better one.

The difference between a wish or a dream and a goal is that the goal has specific features that make it attainable. A well-structured goal must address what you actually want, as opposed to what you don't want or what you're trying to lose or avoid.

Rather than saying, 'I want to lose weight,' talk about what you want instead. For example, 'I want to have a healthy body.' Rather than getting out of debt, talk in terms of having all the bills paid every month and enough extra income each month to pursue your passions and live happily.

Joe watched as Richard opened up his arms and used his hands to emphasize his points. This was a new way of thinking about goal setting.

When you're setting up your goals, it's also vital that you're looking for something specific. If you tell your brain that you want something, it will focus on it, so you need to be clear about what exactly you want.

For example, when you're thinking about buying a certain kind of new car, you'll start noticing a lot of those cars in the streets. How come? Well, because your brain notices more of what you're looking for. So be careful. If you're looking for problems, you'll find them. If you're looking for solutions, you'll find them. And if you're looking for ways to lose twenty-five pounds, you could find my chainsaw!

Richard raised one eyebrow and waited for the audience to settle as they giggled.

Also, the way you define what you want is important. Take the example of the house of your dreams. A lot of people say, 'My goal is to buy the house of my dreams.' Are you sure the goal is to buy the house? Or would you prefer living in the house of your dreams?

The secret is to figure out what result you're after. There's a big difference between buying and living. The first is the process for attaining your goal; the second is the result you're going to get.

You've got to ask good questions, like what will I see, hear and feel when I reach my goal? This will help.

Joe thought about buying a house, and he imagined the whole process of paying for the house and the signing of contracts. When he thought of living in his dream house he felt a thousand times more motivated than when he thought of the buying process. He shook his head and smiled.

When you don't aim towards satisfaction, your brain is aimed towards dissatisfaction. It's looking for faults. But as soon as you put a good voice and a good picture in your mind and focus on what's wonderful about something, you feel better. You need more of a focus like this, because if you think yourself towards pleasure and you think yourself towards success, that's where you'll go.

Joe clenched his hands together. Until now his brain had been focused a lot on what was missing in his life. It seemed obvious that he would be dissatisfied.

You also must think about what you have and don't have control over with regard to your goals. There's no point in having a goal of winning the lottery. You need to focus on a goal that you can control or influence.

Joe fidgeted with his manual. What kind of things was he in control of with respect to achieving his goals?

Now I want you to do an exercise where you begin to design your own future. I want you to find someone to work with and help each other get clear on what you want and ensure that you're thinking about it in the most useful ways. The questions for the exercise are in your manuals.

Joe turned immediately towards Sarah so that he could pair up with her for the exercise. She had leaned over towards him at the same time. Sarah went first. Her goal was to become a best-selling author.

'So, Sarah, what do you want?' Joe looked at her and tried to concentrate on the exercise.

'I want to get my book written and get it onto the best-seller list.'

'OK, how will you know when you've achieved this?'

Sarah's eyes lit up. 'I'll know that I've reached my goal when I see my book in the bookshops of the biggest cities in the world.' She looked happy.

'OK, what about the best-seller list?'

Sarah put her finger to her lips and looked towards the ceiling. 'Actually, I don't care that much about the best-seller list. I'm more interested in having the book translated into as many languages as possible and in knowing that it's been read by thousands of people! Wow. The more I think about this goal, the more excited I get!'

'Great. Now when specifically do you want this to happen?'

'I aim to get it done in the next few months, so, realistically, I want my book in bookshops at the end of this year.'

Joe noted this down and continued. 'That's great. Now, is this goal worth it? You'll need to spend a lot of time writing the book, and therefore you'll miss out on other things. Is that OK with you?'

Sarah paused and pursed her lips. 'Yes, I'm sure it'll be worth it. I won't forget about the other important things in my life, but this is something I really want to do.'

Joe continued with his questions. 'What elements are under your control? What can you do about this?'

She replied thoughtfully, 'I can write the book, review my writing, and have others look at it and give me feedback. I also need to send it to publishers or get an agent, and to market the book as best I can. I can't control whether people buy it, but I can do my best to make it available and well known.'

Joe brought her through the exercise again, discussing it in more and more depth, and at the end her face was beaming with belief. She said that she felt determined and committed to achieving the result. 'That really helped me. I feel far clearer about it now. I actually think I'll be able to do it when I want.' Joe nodded encouragingly.

Joe's turn. Sarah started with the questioning. 'So what do you want?'

Joe put his right hand on his belly. 'I'd like to lose weight.'

Sarah looked at him cheekily. 'OK, well, I don't have my chainsaw here but I can look for one if you like.'

Joe smirked. 'No, smart-ass, I'd prefer to be fit and not so soft around the edges.'

She pressed him. 'What specifically is it to be fit? What would you see, hear and feel that let you know you had that kind of body?'

'I suppose I'd be looking at myself in the mirror and seeing how strong I was. And maybe I'd hear people compliment me on how I looked – I'd be feeling full of energy and healthy.'

'Looking at yourself in the mirror, huh? How incredibly vain.' Sarah teased him again.

Joe's face went slightly red.

'Yeah, well, when you look like I'm going to look, it's a pleasure to do so.'

Sarah grinned. 'OK, Mr Handsome, so is being this fit and strong worth it? What about all that time you'll spend exercising in the gym? What about all that effort you'll have put in?'

Joe thought about the lifestyle he'd need to have to get the body that he wanted. He thought of the food he'd have to eat and the exercise he'd have to do, and he imagined being as healthy as he wanted to be. 'Yes, it will be worth it. I mean, I'm not going to turn into someone obsessed with nuts and berries and twenty-kilometre runs every morning or anything, but I'm going to do whatever it takes to look and feel the way I want.'

'So what's under your control? What can you do about it?'

'Well, most of it is under my control. I just need to find a healthy food plan and exercise regime that works for me. Once

I find it, I just need to follow it. I can hire a personal trainer or find someone to exercise with me. This will help me keep motivated. Then I'll be able to be as fit as I want.'

As Joe had done with Sarah, she brought him through his goal in more detail, and by the end he was feeling highly motivated. She explained to him that she was glad of doing the exercise with him because she also had a similar goal. Joe's eyes widened and he raised his eyebrows.

'But you don't need to lose weight. You are ...' He trailed off without finishing the sentence, afraid of how the compliment might reveal his feelings.

'Thanks, but I know that I do need to,' she insisted. 'Sometimes I'm happy with how I look, but I still have plenty of blah days where I just don't like how I look at all. And when I get like that I can be a nightmare.'

'You mean you can be worse than you already are? Impossible!' Joe joked.

'Ha, ha, smart guy.' She gently smacked him on the arm.

The coffee break arrived, and while Sarah went to get some coffee Joe went outside to enjoy a combination of fresh air and nicotine.

He sparked up and thought about how free he felt to actually move forward in his life. For years his mind had been dominated by memories of all the experiences he'd tried and failed and by all the reasons he hadn't been able to succeed. It had never occurred to him that it was important to focus on what he wanted rather than on his challenges. Now he realized that he should be focusing on the solution rather than on the problem.

He came back and was offered a cup of tea by Teresa. 'How are you doing?' she asked.

'I'm good. That was a cool exercise, getting us focused on the direction our lives are going. I like that.'

'Yes, I know what you mean. So, tell me, when are you going to ask Sarah out?'

'God, is there anyone in here who isn't going to ask me that question? She's already taken.'

'Are you sure?' Teresa asked, her brow furrowed. 'I don't think she is. I've been watching the two of you. It's so cute, the way she's looking at you. And the way she smiles at you ...'

Joe felt his cheeks going red and shook his head sheepishly. He wanted so much to believe Teresa, but he heard his critical voice trying to mock him. Immediately he changed its tone, so it had no impact on him. Another victory for Mickey Mouse. But maybe she was right? He blushed and replied, 'Yeah. We get on well.'

Teresa moved closer to Joe. 'Well, just my advice. I suggest that before you leave today you ask her out or at least find out if she's single. Never have regrets because you didn't ask one question. It's not worth it. Sometimes you have to just go for it and be willing to deal with whatever the universe throws your way.'

Joe changed the subject and as soon as they finished their tea they headed back inside to the auditorium. Sarah was already back in her seat, talking to the woman in front of her. Richard came back onstage.

The power of questions

Now that you've started looking at exactly where you want to go and what direction your life is going in, the next step is to start doing the things you need to do in order to get there.

Where does this lead us? Well, to the fact that the kind of questions we ask ourselves affects the quality of our life.

There's no intrinsically bad question. Neither is there an intrinsically good one, but typically people spend way too much time asking themselves why, and that's often not only useless but also actively harmful.

If you suddenly realized that you were drowning, would you spend time asking yourself why you were drowning? Would you find that kind of question useful at that moment? Of course not. Instead, you'd start asking yourself how you could get out of the water – and as safely and as quickly as possible.

Joe recalled his phone call with Maria. He was looking forward to speaking with her again.

As soon as you ask yourself a question – any question – your mind will actively begin to look for an answer. So if the question is 'Why do I feel this bad?' you'll get plenty of reasons. Thinking about all those reasons will make you feel even worse!

Instead, start asking yourself the kind of questions that will help you improve the quality of your life and see for yourself how that's going to affect you. Now, I want you to take some time and generate some questions with each other that are designed to free your energy and empower you to quickly change the way you perceive problems.

Joe stared blankly at his feet. For the first time during the workshop he found himself unable to come up with anything. Alan came walking down towards his seat and nodded across at him as everyone looked for others to pair up with.

'Hey, Joe, looking for a partner?'

'Yeah, I've no clue where to start with this.'

'Now, just to give you some ideas, when I work with clients coaching them to achieve their goals, there are some questions I ask them. I do so in order to get their brains going in the right direction and help them transform their goals into action. The questions are:

'What do I need to do more of to reach my goal?

'What do I need to do less of to reach my goal?

'What do I need to stop doing to reach my goal?

'What do I need to begin to do to reach my goal?'

Joe thought through each question carefully. He wrote them down and thought about his goal of getting fit. Then, he asked himself these questions in turn:

What do I need to do more of?

Walk more. Avoid the car as much as possible.

What do I need to do less of?

Watch less TV. Eat less pizza and ice cream.

What do I need to stop doing?

Stop smoking right now.

What do I need to begin to do?

Go to the gym. Follow a precise training plan. Be sure to go there three times a week. Buy a book to learn how to eat in a healthy way. Apply these principles to my life.

Alan allowed him some time to do this, and then said, 'Now what kind of questions could you ask to set you off in a better direction?'

Joe furiously wrote down questions.

How can I change?

Why do I want to change?

What will it be like when I have changed?

How can I build the life of my dreams?

Who do I need to be to achieve what I want?

What do I need to learn to create the life I want?

When will I start taking action?

As he wrote down each question, another popped in his head. He didn't notice but Alan began walking away while Joe's head was buried in his notebook. It was only the music from the auditorium sound system that signalled the end of the exercise and drew Joe's attention back to Richard in the centre of the stage.

Now, what I'm trying to get across to you is what builds freedom. You need to have the freedom to feel good more of the time. That's what you need. You need to get bigger, better, bolder, shinier pictures and feel attracted to them. You need to have a whole new selection of voices in your head, useful voices.

Remember that disappointment requires adequate planning. You have to plan ahead of time to be disappointed. But you can also plan other, better feelings to improve your life.

So I want you to start planning for wonderful feelings. And you can start with planning hunger, because it's lunchtime.

These words echoed in Joe's mind – disappointment as something that 'requires adequate planning'. *So true. So true.*

I'm going to give you an earlier-than-usual lunch break and, when you meet me back here, we'll start to put together everything you've been learning.

As Richard walked offstage Joe started walking out the door with Sarah and Teresa. They met Anna, Peter and Ross, and the six of them decided to go for lunch together.

Joe wanted to ask Sarah about her boyfriend. After all, there was a chance that the guy he'd seen in the car the day before wasn't involved with her. He could be a colleague, a friend ... her brother. They sat down in the restaurant, and Sarah went to the ladies'.

Joe was surprised at how animated Anna seemed to be at the table. She was in a really good mood and the defensive stance she had armed herself with on the first day was nowhere to be seen. 'Well, the way I see it, we all have different ways of working, but I've certainly got a lot of useful things I can do with clients to help them.'

Ross seemed to have responded to Anna's change in attitude. 'Yes, Anna, you're naturally talented at working with these techniques. The way you brought me through that exercise yesterday was brilliant. Really cleared some things up for me. I can see why your clients like working with you. Even if you do *Psycho*-analyse them,' Ross joked.

Anna laughed. 'Be careful, or I'll analyse you, Mr Psycho.'

It was nice to see them getting along well at last.

Peter seemed equally upbeat. 'Oh man,' he said to Joe, 'I can't wait to get back to competition. I feel like I've got a real edge the last three days. I'm so psyched up.'

'That's cool,' Joe said. 'I'm happy for you. Keep me informed on how you do, will you?'

Peter nodded and Ross jumped in. 'Yes, we should all stay in touch and hold each other accountable for what our goals are.'

That was a good idea. Before he could agree, they had already divided themselves into pairs. Anna was put with Ross and Joe was put with Peter, while Teresa and Sarah would keep track of each other's progress. Joe grimaced. That was another chance, Joe thought. Another chance to have an excuse to stay in touch with Sarah.

Sarah came back to the table and agreed that holding each other accountable would be a great idea.

Over lunch they talked openly about the course and what it meant for each of them. But Joe was quiet. He sat there pensively, thinking about his past, present and future. What mattered was that he needed to change things now. He needed to build the kind of future that he wanted.

Life had seemed out of control for so long that Joe had resigned himself to accepting the problems he had. But now he had learned tools to control his thoughts and to manage his feelings.

Joe noticed that while Sarah and Peter were in the middle of a conversation she had glanced over in his direction. It almost seemed as if she wanted to talk, to Joe, just the two of them.

Joe's phone vibrated in his pocket. It was a text message. Joe furrowed his brow with surprise when he saw the name. It was Lisa. Why was she texting him? He opened the message. *Joe, please call me. I want to talk to you about something important*. He went outside and lit up a cigarette. He re-read the message. Then he dialled her number. His stomach was in knots. The phone rang only twice before he heard her voice.

'Joe. Joe. It's you.' She sounded half upset and half excited. 'It's so good to finally get to talk to you, Joe.'

'Hi, Lisa. Your message was unexpected.'

'Yes, I know. But I've been thinking a lot about you lately.'

Joe didn't know what to say to that, so he said nothing.

Lisa continued. 'I was actually thinking that we made a good couple. I know we were together only a few months, but …' She trailed off, hoping Joe would start talking.

He did. 'So how's the other guy?' he asked sourly.

'It didn't work out, Joe. I knew it wouldn't, really. I mean, it was just physical. It was nothing like what you and I had together.'

Joe wasn't sure what was going on, what Lisa was asking. Did Lisa want to get back together with him? 'Lisa, why do you want to talk? What are you looking for?' he said impatiently.

'I love you, Joe. I miss you, and I want us to get back together. I'm sorry I made a mistake, but I know we'll be stronger for it. You weren't giving me the attention I deserved, with all your work, and that was wrong, but what I did was even worse. I'm sorry.'

Joe rubbed his hand across his face.

'I'm at a seminar, Lisa. I can't talk now.'

'Will you at least think about talking things over with me again? Please?' Lisa pleaded.

'Eh, OK. I'll think about things.'

Joe hung up the phone, put the cigarette out and went back inside. His mind was racing. He was partly excited and partly angry about hearing from her.

'Wow, Joe, looks like you saw a ghost out there. Are you all right?' Sarah commented as he approached his seat.

'Um, yeah, sorry – I did. The Ghost of Christmas Past,' he responded. Sarah frowned at him curiously. He shrugged and added, 'It's a long story.'

'Well, we're thinking of going for a drink after the course later. Would you be up for it?'

'Sure,' Joe said and smiled.

Joe walked back to the auditorium with Sarah after lunch. She began talking to him about the reasons she'd signed up for the seminar. 'I suppose I'm here because I needed to do something. Last year I was made redundant from my job because they were restructuring. I had applied for more than twenty jobs since then, but I kept getting rejected. This seminar has taught me that maybe I spent far too much time assuming I won't get what I want, because it has been the same with the book. I really want to finish it and get it published, but I've just been imagining it not happening.'

As Joe listened he was surprised that Sarah thought so negatively. She had always come across as being so positive to him in the few days since he had first noticed her.

'Of course, as I said earlier, I definitely want to get fitter and healthier.' She smiled. 'I've decided I'm going to take up Pilates to do so. I need to be able to look at myself in the mirror and like what I see.' Joe wanted to tell her that she was beautiful.

'And don't get me started on guys …'

What did that mean? Did it mean she was single? Was she taken but unhappy? He had no idea what that meant but he decided not to ask her. He didn't want to hear any bad news.

'It's not so bad, really. It's just that sometimes I feel like it's me against the big, bad world. Alone. You know? I'm just tired of living a mundane life. I think I deserve more. Now I know I do. And this course is just what I need to get me to start taking responsibility for my life.'

Joe felt a real connection with Sarah as she spoke honestly about what was on her mind.

'Anyway,' she continued, 'enough of my blah. I just told you because … well, because I get the feeling that you understand what I'm talking about.'

'I know exactly what you're saying.' They talked more about the different ideas they had got from the course.

As they wandered back into the auditorium a few minutes later, Sarah headed back to her seat. Joe was completely absorbed in his thoughts about the course, and about Sarah and Lisa.

He was so absorbed that he didn't notice Alan approaching him. 'You OK, Joe? You seem totally zoned out.'

'Yeah, I'm grand. Just thinking about things and processing what Richard has been saying. It's a lot to take in, you know?'

'Yes, it is a lot to take in, but remember that our brain is capable of far more than we give it credit for. We have the ability to learn multiple languages and encode vast amounts of information. You need to trust yourself more. One of my trainers, John La Valle, used to say, "You are smarter than you think!"'

It was just the application of the knowledge that Joe needed to focus on. And he had to make a few decisions. He thanked Alan again and headed back to his seat, strapping himself in for the afternoon session and for another bout of Richard's words.

Now, earlier I was telling you about Laura. Well, as I helped her create different feelings she began to feel differently about the tasks I gave her. She started to imagine herself talking to people confidently and effortlessly. I had her begin to change her beliefs so that she no longer saw herself as the lonely, depressed lady she had been, and she instead imagined herself as the best version of herself.

She began to look forward to the future, and she started imagining how she wanted her life to turn out differently, and when she thought about it she began to go in a new and fantastic direction. Her whole life turned around once she took control over it and became the controlling element.

Joe nodded along. He could actually take control of his life too.

It's something that you could all do, take control over your life. So we're going on a journey now into your imagination. So just place your feet on the floor, relax your body and allow your eyes to gently close, because what I want you to do now is create some relaxing feelings. When you create relaxing feelings, it helps you to feel better about the future and look at things differently.

Closing his eyes, Joe relaxed more into his seat.

When I did all that stuff with Charlie, what I was getting him to do was to look at things differently. For years he was trapped because of his imagination. All I wanted him to do was to use his imagination to become free.

The Devil's final words to Charlie were, 'Now, Charlie, I want you to turn around to your bedside table, and you'll see a book.'

Charlie turned and saw this book with a big red cover on it.

The voice continued, 'This is my book, and I want you to read it and do the best job you can and never mention my name again to anyone.'

So Charlie turned to read the book. The title on it said *Insurance Sales Manual*, and there was a business card there with his name on it.

You see, I had a few contacts in an insurance sales company, and since Charlie's background had been sales I asked them would they do me a favour and give him a job. Actually, he became one hell of an employee! In fact, he sold more than a million dollars' worth of insurance in less than a year, and that requires tremendous motivation.

Charlie went back to having some sort of life. Now instead of being stuck in a hospital and trapped in his own thoughts, he had a chance for a better life.

In the absence of hope, sometimes you need to create it.

I've found faster and easier ways to help people take charge of their lives, but the key is still the same. You have to be absolutely relentless.

Feelings of determination grew inside of Joe. He could relate to Charlie. Even though they might have had different problems, Joe had his own demons that had pushed him down from inside his own head. He had a voice that he had fought against for far too long.

Once you start becoming happier and taking more control over your life, you need to appreciate things more. Instead of looking at what you don't have, enjoy what you do have now, so that if you have a bit more you'll enjoy it that much more.

I knew somebody who decided that he was going to retire a multimillionaire. He had a family and rarely saw his kids. He hardly even saw his wife. Then he retired really rich, and three months later he died. The minute he had nothing to do, he just went nuts. It was too painful for him sitting around the house all day, tapping his foot. He didn't propel himself into a future that was more and more exquisite. Plus, he had wasted all that time trying to achieve only one goal – to become rich, when in reality he needed to just appreciate more of what was going on in his life. That's true wealth.

All the wonderful things Joe had in his own life came flooding into his mind. His loving sister Maria and even the enjoyable parts of his job. He thought about the course he'd attended and the new friends he'd met during it.

To me, it's a good idea to remind yourself of all the horrible things that might happen if you don't do what will take you in the best direction in life.

Sometimes, even thinking of a horrible future can give you a boost so that you're propelled toward what you want. Then, you need to imagine having what you want in vivid detail and do the things you need to do to achieve your dreams.

Joe had assumed that you were supposed to always motivate yourself by thinking of what you want to achieve. However, now he considered what would happen if he stayed where he was and as opposed to what would happen if he did achieve his goal. This made him feel even more determined to achieve it.

You can be motivated in two basic ways, or drives. One is the urge to move away from pain. The other is the compelling desire to move towards pleasure.

It's just like the young woman I worked with, who survived the terrorist attack. She learned to do something absolutely necessary. She learned to change her focus from the problems of the past to the opportunities of the future.

She had to realize that the more she reminded herself of the trauma, the worse she would feel, and that when she started getting into the habit of thinking about the future instead, she would feel amazing. In fact, a few months later she wrote me an e-mail to thank me for the exercise that I brought her through. She learned to propel herself away from her negative feelings and towards feeling hopeful about the future.

When you look vividly at what could be possible and you decide to make it happen, you can create amazing things. Think about it. At one time there were no buildings on this planet. Now there are millions. There was no way to reach people on the other side of the world. Now we can get on planes and fly there in less than a day.

DAY THREE: HOW TO CREATE THE LIFE YOU WANT

We can communicate with people and see them while we talk to them over the internet from continent to continent. The possibilities are endless for you. You can create the life you want once you are free.

Freedom. All the stories Richard had told, all his experiences, were about freedom. These people were trapped in their own way of thinking, just as Joe had been. Now they were free, just as Joe could be. He felt a rush of excitement about the future.

So tonight, while you sleep and dream, your mind will begin to reflect on all I've been talking about for the last three days and on the concept of personal freedom.

My life's work is about helping people unlock the chains of negative feelings and limiting beliefs and enabling them to be free to create the life they want.

It's like I was saying on day one. Many people feel trapped by the past, but they aren't really trapped. They're just practising a habit of feeling bad. A lot of people destroy their present with their past. They take the bad things that have happened to them and believe it will determine their future.

I want you to leave here today and learn from your past. I want you to see your present as an opportunity for you to do some new things, and I want you to look forward to a future that you can create that's full of possibilities.

When I went around to the mental hospitals with Virginia Satir, I was able to help a lot of those people because I believed it was possible to help them.

Once you believe that something is possible, your world will become richer. Then you'll be free to be who you're capable of being and do what you really are capable of doing. In life, you must always remember that you are free to change the way you think, free to change the way you feel and free to design the kind of life you want. You must take charge of your destiny. And always remember to act as if you're the controlling element of your life. When you do, you will be.

Richard enjoyed a standing ovation when he finished. Joe got to his feet and applauded. He wanted to acknowledge the man who had delivered to him the realization of freedom.

Sarah was one of the first in line to get a picture with Richard. Joe decided against going up to thank him. There was already a long line there. He walked towards the exit, where he met Alan.

'Alan, listen … I just want to say thanks so much for everything. You've been a great help to me. I'd like to stay in touch, if that's OK.'

'Sure.' Alan beamed and handed Joe his business card. 'Give me a shout any time and let me know what's going on for you, OK?'

Joe looked at the business card. 'Yes, I will. I'm not going up to Richard now. But …' Joe paused and looked back at the stage where Richard was signing autographs.

Alan jumped in. 'I know. Like he always says, "Don't repay me with compliments; repay me with actions." Make this seminar worth it, Joe.'

'I will,' Joe said, surprising himself with his certainty. He shook Alan's hand, and then went looking for the rest of the gang.

Sarah returned from the front, looking elated. She showed Joe the photograph she had taken with Richard. She and Joe stood talking for a while until Anna, Ross, Peter and Teresa found them, and they all left the conference room together, heading for the nearby pub. As they left, Joe reached inside his pocket and took the cigarettes out. He looked at them for one last time and dropped them in the bin. Joe turned again to see the beautiful face of Sarah beside him. She was waiting for him to walk with her.

On the way into the pub they got talking about their favourite foods. She seemed like a real connoisseur, yet he barely knew how to hold a fork. When she talked about her favourite salad her face lit up with excitement. He teased her about this, and then she reminded him of his 'obsession with checking himself out in the mirror'. They continued to tease each other and to talk about Richard, about the seminar and the different things they would do differently in their lives.

They planned on staying for one drink. Soon Anna made her excuses and said her good-byes. As if the others had planned it, they each left one by one, next Ross and Teresa, and soon after, Peter. Now it was just Joe and Sarah chatting and joking and laughing. Joe felt as though they had known each other for ever.

Joe was building up to ask her about her boyfriend. He was stumbling around the topic, and before he had a chance to bring it up the man who had driven her the previous day walked into the pub. Joe was suddenly aware of how close to Sarah he was sitting and his body clammed up as he sat back.

His face went red and he shuffled in his seat. As he began to fidget with his bottle of beer, he instinctively became aware of what he was doing and took his feelings of discomfort and embarrassment and he spun them in the opposite direction. *What's the most useful thing to do right now?* He remembered what Alan had said: *Focus on feeling good and making others feel good as well.*

The man walked in and kissed Sarah on both cheeks. She seemed delighted to see him. Joe stood, smiled, and shook the guy's hand. Sarah introduced him as Ted. 'Hello, Joe.' He turned to Sarah and said, 'Well, Sarah, where have you been hiding this gorgeous creature!' It took Joe a couple of seconds to figure out that Ted was talking about him. And then Joe smiled. Sarah and Ted were just friends.

The three of them chatted for a few minutes more. Ted was a funny guy. He regaled them with stories of his recent trip abroad with his boyfriend. Joe was enjoying the company, but he also knew that he had a question to ask. Then his phone vibrated again. It was another message. From Lisa. Her message read: *Will you meet me tomorrow to talk about us?* Joe texted back: *Yes. 1 p.m. The coffee shop we always went to.*

He turned back to Sarah just as Ted was making his way to the bar. Joe decided that it was time. He imagined himself feeling strong and confident. He spun good feelings through his body. He challenged any negative beliefs that tried to stop him. He smiled and said, 'Sarah, I was wondering if you might like to go out with me some time for a drink.'

Sarah's face was straight. She stared back at him without saying anything. After what felt to Joe like a lifetime, she replied. 'We're already out for a drink. You mean on a date?'

Joe nodded apprehensively, biting his lip.

Sarah blinked hard, flicked her hair out of her eyes and then finally answered.

Chapter 5

AFTER THE WORKSHOP: THE MOST IMPORTANT QUESTION

Three months after the seminar had finished, Joe was cleaning up the paperwork on his desk when he came across the workshop manual. He spotted a phone number for Peter on the front page. He went to his wallet and took out Alan's business card. *Maybe I should give them a call?*

'Hey, Peter, it's Joe from the course with Richard Bandler. What's up, buddy?'

'Hey, Joe. Great to hear from ya, bro. How are you? All is fantastic with me. I made it. I made it to the European Championships. I beat my best time and qualified.'

'That's terrific news. Congratulations! I'm so happy for you. You're sticking to your plan, then?'

'Yes, it really has worked well for me. I'm going to give it my best shot. So how's life with you?'

'I'm doing good. I'm back at the gym. I have lost nearly a stone and am feeling full of energy. And I haven't smoked a cigarette since the seminar. I have my down moments from time to time, of course, but those are now few and far between!'

'Man, that brilliant square is so amazing. I feel at my best whenever I use it. Ross really helped me out with that one. He seems to be doing pretty well. I haven't heard from Teresa but I believe Sarah got a publisher for her book. Have you talked to Alan since the course?'

'No, but I'm going to give him a call now and catch up.'

'Well, tell him I said hi.'

Joe promised he would. They chatted for a few minutes more. He enjoyed catching up.

Joe dialled Alan's number. 'Hey, Joe, great to hear from you. How are things?'

Joe spoke about what had happened in his life during the previous three months and the news he had just heard from Peter.

'Things are great, Alan. Obviously there have been ups and downs since the course, but I've made so much progress. I am feeling great at the moment and am a lot happier with myself. I guess I'm learning to stop being so critical of myself and I'm believing in myself a lot more. I've met more people too and feel a lot more confident with others. Thanks so much for all your help.'

Alan was delighted. 'That's so great, Joe. This is only the beginning of a whole new chapter in your life.'

'I think it is. By the way, I have a quick question for you. Although work is much easier to handle than it has ever been, my heart still isn't in it. I want to change jobs, but I am struggling to find out what to do. Do you have any suggestions?'

'The first thing to do is to remember to stay true to your values.'

'My values?' Joe asked.

'Yes. I sent you a letter after the course. It was in a gold envelope. Did you get it?'

'Wait a minute.' Joe searched through the pile in front of him and saw lots of unopened mail that he'd deemed not to be urgent. He soon found the envelope. 'Yes, got it. Must have got lost in the non-essentials of this week,' he said, slightly embarrassed.

'Well, check it out. It's essential and will help you get your mind clear about what to do.'

Joe turned the envelope over in his hands. It glistened against the lamp at the side of the table. When he had finished the call, Joe opened the envelope. Inside was a letter:

Dear Joe,

You have successfully completed a three-day course in personal freedom with Dr Richard Bandler. This, however, is where the real fun starts.

In life, you will have good things happen and bad things happen. You can't always control what happens, but you can always control how you deal with it.

Learning about personal freedom allows you to feel the way you want to feel and create the kinds of feelings that allow you to create a more wonderful life. To enjoy your freedom, you must remember to ask yourself one more question. Ask this question before making important decisions and before defining your goals. The question is:

What are the most important things in your life right now?

Answer this question and make sure that you always have the answer clear. It will keep you aligned with your inner values. This way your decisions will always support what's most important to you.

I wish you the very best life possible. I hope you decide to choose freedom.

Alan

Joe read over the letter a second time and focused on the question. Then his phone rang. He looked at the caller name and smiled. Maria. He arranged to meet up with her for a walk and a chat soon. They had been spending a lot of time together in the last few weeks.

After the call, Joe looked out of the kitchen window. Maybe it was because he had just spoken to Maria or maybe it was because he had changed the way he had thought about himself in the last few months, but he could not help but think about his mother. She had always told him that he was special and that he was a free spirit. He hoped she was looking down on him now. The question in the letter buzzed around his head. He realized that he had found an answer.

It was the people in his life who were the most important ... including himself.

The sound of the doorbell turned Joe's attention away from the window. He ran towards the door and pulled it open quickly.

A huge smile stretched across his face. It was his girlfriend. She jumped into his arms and hugged him. He kissed her sweetly on the lips. Joe looked into her eyes.

'Well, hello, Sarah.'

Chapter 6

JOE'S JOURNAL

Notes from the workshop

Day One

Personal freedom is the ability to feel what you want so that the chains of fear, sadness and hate are broken. These chains are made up of negative feelings, limiting beliefs and destructive behaviours.

A lot of people have had bad things happen to them, but instead of being glad that it's not happening now, they go through it over and over in their heads, so that their present is destroyed by their past.

Many people feel trapped by the past, but they aren't really trapped. They're just practising a habit of feeling bad.

We always have the choice of:

Taking our past and limiting our future

or:

Taking our past and building a better future

NLP is about teaching people how to make it so that when they look at their past they learn from it. They avoid suffering because of it.

Life is not about remembering and reliving unpleasantness from the past but about going forward to look at life as the adventure it can be.

Maybe reality isn't what you think it is. Maybe whatever you think becomes your reality.

Tragedy exists only in the mind as a terrible memory. A memory is just a representation of an experience.

When you change the way you represent an experience, you change how you feel about the experience.

The one thing in life that you can control is the inside of your head. Alan's example: If someone went into your house and painted horrible pictures on your walls, you wouldn't leave them there, would you? No, of course not. You would paint over them. Then why leave bad ideas inside your head? Unwanted negative images or horrible voices … there's no point.

If you don't do it, it won't work.

Day Two

If you take charge of your beliefs, you take charge of your life.

Problems don't exist independently of human beings; they don't exist in the universe at large. They exist in our perceptions and understandings.

Your beliefs can either trap you or set you free.

Whatever you believe will determine what you decide to do. If you truly want to change, the first step is to believe 100 percent that you can and that you will.

Along the way, you built a belief in the kind of person that you were. Maybe that's the person you thought you were, but now if you change that belief you can begin to believe in yourself as the kind of person that you want to be.

By believing that change can't be easy, we prevent it from being so.

When you're at your best, what are you capable of?

Just because people haven't found a way doesn't mean that there isn't one. If you believe with every part of you that there is a way, then you'll probably find one.

Believe that you can achieve what you want, and you'll set yourself free to achieve it.

There are beliefs about what you can do and what you can't do.

There are also beliefs about who you are and who you are not.

What you believe determines how you act.

How you act determines what results you get.

The results you get determine what your beliefs are.

Beliefs –> Actions –> Results –> Beliefs

Happy and successful people have a lot of useful beliefs about themselves, the goals they want to achieve and the resources they have to achieve it. They believe they can have what they want, and they believe they deserve it. This is what allows them to take massive action, which gets them results.

Your beliefs limit or expand your world.

Day Three

If you're looking for problems, you'll find them.

As soon as you ask yourself a question, your mind will actively begin to look for an answer. So if the question is why do I feel this bad … you'll get plenty of reasons.

Looking for the reasons you're feeling so bad might not be the wisest idea. Instead, start asking yourself the kind of questions that will help you improve the quality of your life and see for yourself how that's going to affect you.

Four questions to transform goals into actions:

What do I need to do more of to reach my goal?
What do I need to do less of to reach my goal?
What do I need to stop doing to reach my goal?
What do I need to begin to do to reach my goal?

Remember: disappointment requires adequate planning.

Instead of looking at what you don't have, enjoy what you do have now. This helps you to propel yourself, step by step, into a future that's more and more exquisite.

When you create relaxing feelings, it helps you look at things differently.

Once you believe that something is possible, your world will open up.

In the absence of hope, sometimes you need to create it.

Act as if you're the controlling element of your life. When you do, you will be.

Epilogue

SHARE THE MESSAGE, SHARE YOUR STORY

This book teaches you to observe the way you think and challenge your limiting, unsupportive beliefs. It enables you to raise your consciousness.

We wrote this book because we believe we have a message that everyone needs to hear.

You can choose freedom. You can take charge of your life. This is a user's guide towards using NLP to do just that.

As each individual raises his or her consciousness, the world raises its consciousness, moving from fear to freedom. We therefore ask you to share this message of consciousness and empowerment with others. Get this message out to as many people as possible – family, friends and colleagues.

Our dream is that, one book, one course, one person at a time, we can change the world in a positive way. We ask for your support in making this dream a reality. Together we can create a movement towards a happier world.

We hope to meet you in person in the future. Meanwhile we can connect online at

www.nlpmovement.com

Here you can find, read and share true personal stories about life experiences on personal freedom, including your own. We want to know how the ideas of personal freedom have changed your life. We encourage you to share your stories with us. Spread the word and change the world!

All the best,

Richard Bandler, Alessio Roberti and Owen Fitzpatrick

RESOURCES

NLP Techniques

NLP has become known for offering a wide range of techniques for changing and improving our personal and professional lives.

In this book, we presented some of them as used by Richard and Alan to help the participants of the course. Indeed, we could have written another book just to explain the language patterns and NLP techniques they both used during the story.

But instead, we decided to provide you, the reader, with an special online resource where you can find videos and written explanations of NLP techniques. Just go and visit

www.nlpmovement.com

to get free tips and access to really useful videos now.

See you there!

Alessio Roberti and Owen Fitzpatrick

Recommended Reading

Bandler, Richard, *Using Your Brain for a Change*, Real People Press, Durango, CO, 1985

—, *Magic in Action*, Meta Publications, Capitola, CA, 1985

—, *The Adventures of Anybody*, Meta Publications, Capitola, CA, 1993

—, *Time for a Change*, Meta Publications, Capitola, CA, 1993

—, *Get the Life You Want*, HarperElement, London, 2008

—, *Make Your Life Great*, HarperElement, London, 2010

Bandler, Richard, Delozier, Judith, and Grinder, John, *Patterns of the Hypnotic Techniques of Milton H. Erickson, Volume 2*, Meta Publications, Capitola, CA, 1977

Bandler, Richard, and Grinder, John, *Frogs into Princes*, Real People Press, Capitola, CA, 1979

—, *Patterns of the Hypnotic Techniques of Milton H. Erickson, Volume 1*, Meta Publications, Capitola, CA, 1975

—, *The Structure of Magic*, Meta Publications, Capitola, CA, 1975

—, *The Structure of Magic, Volume 2*, Meta Publications, Capitola, CA, 1975

—, *Trance-formations*, Real People Press, Durango, CO, 1980

Bandler, Richard, and Fitzpatrick, Owen, *Conversations with Richard Bandler*, Health Communications, Deerfield Beach, FL, 2009

Bandler, Richard, and LaValle, John, *Persuasion Engineering*, Meta Publications, Capitola, CA, 1996

RESOURCES

Bandler, Richard, and McDonald, Will, *An Insider's Guide to Submodalities*, Meta Publications, Capitola, CA, 1989

Bandler, Richard, Roberti, Alessio, and Fitzpatrick, Owen, *The Ultimate Introduction to NLP: How to Build a Successful Life*, HarperElement, London, 2012

Bandler, Richard, and Thompson, Garner, *The Secrets of Being Happy: The Technology of Health, Hope and Harmony*, IM Press, 2011

Fitzpatrick, Owen, *The Charismatic Edge: The Art of Captivating and Compelling Communication*, Gill & MacMillan, Dublin, 2013

Fitzpatrick, Owen, *Not Enough Hours: The Secret to Making Every Second Count*, Poolbeg Press, Dublin, 2009

Wilson, Robert Anton, *Prometheus Rising*, New Falcon Publications, Tempe, AZ, 1983

—, *Quantum Psychology*, New Falcon Publications, Tempe, AZ, 1990

DVD and CD Products

Bandler, Richard, *DHE*, CD, 2000

—, *The Art and Science of Nested Loops*, DVD, 2003

—, *Persuasion Engineering*, DVD, 2006

—, *Personal Enhancement Series*, CD, 2010

La Valle, John, *NLP Practitioner Set*, CD, 2009

These and many more DVDs and CDs, both hypnotic and from Richard's seminars, are available from www.nlpstore.com.

Bandler, Richard, *Adventures in Neuro Hypnotic Repatterning*, DVD set and PAL-version videos, 2002
—, *Thirty Years of NLP: How to Live a Happy Life*, DVD set, 2003

These and other products by Richard Bandler are available from Matrix Essential Training Alliance, www.meta-nlp.co.uk; e-mail: enquiries@meta-nlp.co.uk; phone +44 (0)1749 871126; fax +44 (0)1749 870714

Fitzpatrick, Owen, *Love in Your Life*, Hypnosis CD, 2004
—, *Adventures in Charisma*, DVD set, 2008
—, *Performance Boost*, Hypnosis CD, 2011
—, *Confidence Boost*, Hypnosis CD, 2011

Available from www.nlp.ie.

Fitzpatrick, Owen, et al, *The Online Charisma Training Academy*, Online Video & Audio, 2013

Available from www.charismatrainingacademy.com

Websites

www.nlpmovement.com
www.richardbandler.com
www.purenlp.com
www.coach.tv

RESOURCES

www.nlp.ie
www.nlp.mobi
www.nlpcoach.com
www.owenfitzpatrick.com
www.theultimateintroductiontonlp.com
www.charismatrainingacademy.com

THE SOCIETY OF NEURO-LINGUISTIC PROGRAMMING™

Richard Bandler Licensing Agreement

The Society of Neuro-Linguistic Programming™ is set up for the purpose of exerting quality control over those training programs, services and materials claiming to represent the model of Neuro-Linguistic Programming (NLP). The seal below indicates Society Certification and is usually advertised by Society approved trainers. When you purchase NLP products and seminars, ask to see this seal. This is your guarantee of quality.

It is common experience for many people, when they are introduced to NLP and first begin to learn the technology, to be cautious and concerned with the possible uses and misuses.

As a protection for you and for those around you, the Society of NLP™ now requires participants to sign a licensing agreement which guarantees that those certified in this technology will use it with the highest integrity.

It is also a way to ensure that all the training you attend is of the highest quality and that your trainers are up to date with the constant evolution of the field of Neuro-Linguistic Programming and Design Human Engineering®, etc.

For a list of recommendations, go to:

- http://www.NLPInstitutes.com
- http://www.NLPTrainers.com

The Society of NLP™
NLP Seminars Group International
PO Box 424
Hopatcong, NJ 07843, USA
Tel: (973) 770-3600
Website: www.purenlp.com

Copyright 1994–2013 The Society of NLP™ and Richard Bandler

ABOUT THE AUTHORS

Dr Richard Bandler

Dr Richard Bandler is the co-founder of Neuro-Linguistic Programming and the creator of Design Human Engineering® and Neuro-Hypnotic Repatterning™.

For the last forty years Dr Bandler has been one of the most important contributors to the field of personal change. A mathematician, philosopher, teacher, artist and composer, he has created a legacy of books, videos and audios that have changed therapy and education forever.

Hundreds of thousands of people, many of them therapists, have studied Dr Bandler's life's work at more than 600 institutes around the world.

A widely acclaimed keynote speaker and workshop leader, he is the author of more than a dozen books, including *Get the*

Life You Want, *Make Your Life Great* and *Using Your Brain for a Change*, and co-author of *Persuasion Engineering®*, *The Ultimate Introduction to NLP*, *The Secrets of Being Happy* and *Conversations with Richard Bandler*.

For more information on Richard Bandler's workshops and seminars visit www.richardbandler.com.

Alessio Roberti

Alessio Roberti is the 'International Director of Business Coaching' for the Society of NLP, the largest NLP organization in the world.

Alessio is a licensed 'Master Trainer' of NLP and has trained more than 60,000 participants so far.

He has been studying Dr Richard Bandler's work for more than twenty years. He also attended Harvard Business School and Oxford Business School.

He has coached presidents, CEOs, top executives and owners of some of the most important companies worldwide, in many industries.

Alessio also teaches 'Linguistic Intelligence' at the Hotel Business School in the Master in 'Five Stars Hotel Management'.

He is the co-author, with Dr Bandler and Owen Fitzpatrick, of the book *The Ultimate Introduction to NLP*, which has been translated into seven languages.

You can reach Alessio at www.coach.tv.

ABOUT THE AUTHORS

Owen Fitzpatrick

Owen Fitzpatrick is an international speaker and psychologist. He is the co-author of *Conversations with Richard Bandler* and *The Ultimate Introduction to NLP* and the author of *The Charismatic Edge: The Art of Captivating and Compelling Communication* and *Not Enough Hours: The Secret to Making Every Second Count.*

Owen also works with billionaires and Olympic athletes, helping them to perform at their very best. He is an authority in the area of charisma and motivation and he regularly delivers keynote speeches and corporate training on this topic and has shared the stage with such names as Sir Richard Branson.

As well as having a Master's in applied psychology, Owen has studied strategic negotiation at Harvard Business School and is a qualified psychotherapist and hypnotherapist. He is the co-founder of the Irish Institute of NLP. Owen also achieved the accolade of becoming the youngest-ever licensed 'Master Trainer' of NLP in the world, aged just 23.

Owen has travelled from Colombia to Japan and from Italy to Thailand and trained people in more than twenty-three countries worldwide in how to enhance their lives and improve their businesses.

You can find more information on Owen at www.owenfitzpatrick.com or www.nlp.ie.